Praise for *Money Players*

"Congratulations to Marc Isenberg for producing his brilliant work *Money Players*. Issues that have plagued athletes for years are presented and discussed in a straightforward and easy-to-understand format."
—**Gene Washington, director of football operations, National Football League**

"*Money Players* is the best book I have read for college and pro athletes in my 30 years in this business. The book is that good. It should be on every athlete's reading list and every parent/advisor should read it, too. I intend to give it out to recruits and their families."
—**Tony Agnone, football agent**

"With great clarity and inescapable logic, Marc Isenberg has produced the definitive 'game plan' for pro athletes wishing for financial success and security. If you want to avoid the pitfalls and mistakes that have plagued so many young professionals, by all means take a good, hard look at *Money Players*."
—**Dan Guerrero, Director of Athletics, UCLA**

"There is so much wisdom in this book it should be handed to every major college basketball or football player in exchange for signing a letter of intent. It is direct, honest and beautifully organized. There is sound advice about how to handle money, how to recognize trouble and how to avoid relying on people who place their own interests first—and it does not just come from Marc Isenberg, but from sports veterans on all sides of the table."
—**Mike DeCourcy, senior writer, *Sporting News***

"I truly respect Marc Isenberg for his thoughtful approach to the problems facing big-time sports. He is as honest and tenacious as they come. Marc doesn't just complain about a corrupt system; he offers thoughtful solutions. If you are a college or professional athlete, or if you care about athletes, you have to read *Money Players*."
—**Sonny Vaccaro, lecturer, former athletic shoe company executive**

"*Money Players* is a must-read for any athlete wishing to succeed in college or professional sports. Marc Isenberg captures the essence of what every prospective high-level athlete is confronted with today. The key philosophies and strategies discussed in *Money Players* ensure that athletes are financially sound when their playing days are over."
—**Jeffrey Moorad, CEO & General Partner, Arizona Diamondbacks, former sports agent**

"Marc's analysis in *Money Players* is as comprehensive as you will find anywhere. This should be required reading for any college student with professional sports or management aspirations."
—**Bill Duffy, CEO, BDA Sports Management**

"Athletes and those close to them can learn a lifetime's worth of financial lessons by reading Marc's book. Important insights and financial rules for professional athletes to live by are set out clearly in this easily accessible, example-filled book."
—**Ken Shropshire, Director, Wharton Sports Business Initiative, co-author, *The Business of Sports Agents***

"*Money Players* provides a road map for athletes to take responsibility for every aspect of their careers, and to embrace the concept of being engaged and in charge of their career path. One often hears the excuse, 'There's no handbook for dealing with this situation.' Now, with *Money Players*, there truly is a handbook for athletes, and they should take advantage of it."
—**Jay Bilas, ESPN**

"The unwritten rules are now written. An excellent book to help professional athletes take charge of their lives. An excellent resource to help professional athletes keep their hard-earned money working for them—and not others."
—**Darren Rovell, CNBC Sports Business Reporter**

"College athletes do not get compensated, but millions of dollars are still at stake. Marc educates young players about these issues at the most opportune time, when habits and relationships are forming. For those athletes who have a legitimate opportunity to play professional sports, *Money Players* is a key resource."
—**Reggie Minton, Deputy Executive Director, National Assn. of Basketball Coaches (NABC)**

"Well-written and practical, *Money Players* is a tremendous educational tool for every college athletics program. It is comprehensive and filled with real-life stories that help our student-athletes stay on track with NCAA rules and make smart decisions entering professional careers."
—**Judy Van Horn, associate athletic director/senior women's administrator, University of Michigan**

"Marc Isenberg, who has long been a tireless advocate for both professional and amateur athletes, has put together a well researched, extremely informative book. It is clearly a must read for any professional athlete, but it also contains practical, smart advice for the regular guy as well."
—**Seth Davis, writer, *Sports Illustrated*, commentator, CBS Sports**

"Marc's book is an essential guide for all current and aspiring professional athletes and their families. *Money Players* provides a detailed and lively account about the business side of professional sports."
—**Keenan McCardell, NFL player**

"Marc Isenberg offers practical advice to young athletes that is badly needed but hard to find. Information is the best friend of any individual considering a career in professional athletics. *Money Players* is a very valuable source of helpful, unbiased information."
—**Tom Hansen, Commissioner, Pacific-10 Conference**

"Marc Isenberg is America's most magnanimous guy. Instead of railing at the inequities of a system that makes outside linebackers far richer than guidance counselors, he accepts it and moves on. The Greg Odens and Kevin Durants of the world should thank Marc for providing them with this all-encompassing handbook for their experience."
—**Jim Lampley, HBO Sports**

"Marc Isenberg has worked tirelessly to improve the lives of athletes, both during their playing careers years and beyond. Marc's latest book, *Money Players*, is a great service and a must-read for all athletes (and those guiding them) who want to protect themselves from making bad and ill-informed decisions."
—**Dale Brown, head basketball coach, Louisiana State University, 1972-1997**

"Author Marc Isenberg provides athletes with the information they need to advocate for themselves in a system that sometimes treats them like commodities rather than human beings. From lessons in personal finance to sports labor history to NCAA rules to basic rules of professionalism, this book is a great primer on how athletes can succeed in the business of sport."
—**Dr. Ellen J. Staurowsky, professor and graduate chair, Dept. of Sport Management and Media, Ithaca College**

"*Money Players* stresses the long-term value of getting a meaningful education and degree. While this book can prepare a select few for a professional sports career, it provides excellent counsel to all student-athletes pursuing a productive, successful and meaningful life. I encourage every college football coach and anyone else who works with athletes to read—and share—this book."
—**Grant Teaff, executive director, American Football Coaches Assn. (AFCA)**

Money Players is a great equalizer for athletes who do not want to be taken advantage of by unethical representation. Reading Marc's book increases the chance that a current or future professional athlete selects ethical and competent agent.
—**Darren Heitner, founder, SportsAgentBlog.com**

This book is intended primarily for current and future professional athletes as well as those who influence, advise, and work on their behalf:

★ **Parents** Older and hopefully wiser, most parents are dedicated to the best interests of their sports prodigies. They can shoulder some of the burdens of dealing with the business side of professional sports. If they are not familiar with the business of sports, or with business in general, they must guard against the same mistakes that inexperienced athletes often make…the very mistakes described in this book.

★ **Advisers** such as coaches, relatives or family friends who have a parental or mentoring relationship to an athlete.

★ **Agents, lawyers, investment advisers and others who work with or want to work with professional athletes.** Too many unqualified and/or unethical people are eager to represent professional athletes and vie for a "piece of the action." This contributes to the negative public perception about sports agents. Athletes need competent legal and financial professionals with high integrity. This book helps such professionals by describing what an intelligent and informed athlete wants from relationships with them. Agents who hound athletes, who provide benefits in violation of NCAA rules, and who do not provide objective counsel to college-eligible athletes considering turning pro will not benefit from *Money Players*. Then again, they are probably not reading it.

MONEY PLAYERS

To Eric —
    Thank you for supporting my
efforts! Enjoy!

          Best Regards,
          Marc

Go Eagles!

MONEY PLAYERS

A Guide to Success in
Sports, Business & Life
for Current and Future Pro Athletes

Marc Isenberg

Agame
Publishing

Los Angeles

Money Players: A Guide for Current and Future Pro Athletes to Succeed in Sports, Business & Life

Published by A-Game, LLC
PO Box 34867
Los Angeles, CA 90034

Cover design by Rich Goodnight (www.goodnight.com)
Book design by Jennifer Wilson (www.jenniferwilsondesigns.com)

Visit www.a-game.com for more resources.
Visit moneyplayers.typepad.com to read author's blog.

Cataloging-in-publication data
Isenberg, Marc, 1967-
Money players: a guide for current and future pro athletes to succeed in sports, business & life/ Marc Isenberg
p. cm.
ISBN 978-0-9666764-1-9
1. College athletes—Education—United States. 2. College athletes—United States—Life skills guides. 3. Professional athletes—United States—Life skills guides. 4. Professional sports—Vocational guidance—United States. 5. Sports—Economic aspects. I. Title.
GV734.I84 2007
796/.023

DEDICATION

This book is dedicated to those who helped shape sports and society:

Jackie Robinson, Muhammad Ali, Henry Aaron, Spencer Haywood, Curt Flood and Marvin Miller, who fought for freedom and fairness, and Pete Rozelle and Michael Jordan, who revolutionized the business of sports.

They changed the game, on and off the court. Today's professional athletes are the direct benefactors of their work and sacrifices.

ACKNOWLEDGMENTS

Writing this book has been an incredible team effort. The enormous contributions of others helped elevate this book project to a truly "A" Game level.

Rick Rhoads willingly offered to edit *Money Players—the booklet*, which I originally envisioned as a short guide to help college athletes make a successful transition to professional sports. Of course, that evolved into *Money Players—the book*, which Rick not only edited but also helped write. I am grateful for his dedication and mentorship—and the support of his great wife, Peggy. **Debbie Spander** agreed to be my wife, not my sports legal scholar and editor. Yet she excels in all three capacities. She is also an accomplished sports and entertainment lawyer. Thank you from the bottom of my heart. USC Annenberg School professor **Jeff Fellenzer** would not settle for my "B" game. He worked tirelessly to edit the book, not once, but two times. So thank you twice. **Ryan Nece** wrote the foreword and gave his time generously to explain his world of professional football. **Joel Corry** helped plant the seed for this book when we were college teammates, and helped bring it to fruition through thousands (no exaggeration) of conversations and e-mails. Research assistant **Preetom Bhattacharya** helped compile information on leagues and players associations. **Lee Schwartz** offered brutally honest—and appreciated—criticism. **Steve "The Closer" Krone** lived up to his billing with one last, critical read-thru. **Jennifer Wilson** (page layout) and **Rich Goodnight** (cover) went above and beyond to design the book. **Sebastian Conley** and **Rob Osborne** helped me conserve words—one cartoon is worth at least 1,000 words. I am fortunate to have two great parents **Daryl Holtz Isenberg** and **Howard Isenberg**, and in-laws **Art** and **Liz Spander**.

UCLA has been become my *de facto* research lab. I thank Dan Guerrero, Petrina Long, Bob Field, Rich Herczog, and former student-athletes Tyus Edney, Donnie Edwards, Richard Petruska and Baron Davis. Michael Farrell and Barry Bekkedam, my partners at Ballamor Capital, have been supportive of my efforts to educate athletes about money. I am grateful to a number of people who shared their expertise, including Rachel Newman-Baker and Deana Garner (NCAA), Marvin Miller, Hal Biagas and Mark Levin (players associations), Gene Washington and Stu Jackson (leagues), Dick Greene (taxes and estate planning), Tony Agnone, Ralph Cindrich, Jack Mills and Jim Tanner (agents), and Dale Brown, John Wooden and Marvin Miller (rabble-rousing and inspiration).

Thanks to the growing number of people cover the business of professional sports, particularly Liz Mullen (*The Sports Business Journal*), Stephan Fatsis (*The Wall Street Journal*), Darren Rovell (CNBC), Ken Shropshire and Andrew Zimbalist.

Special thanks to: Professor Robin Keller, Reggie Minton, Jim Haney, Grant Teaff, Jerry Wainwright, David and Dana Pump, the Fryes (Channing, Tom and Karen), Ellen Staurowsky, Fred Claire, Jeffrey Evans, Jeff Bacon, Michael Salmon, Brian Taylor, Glenn Goodstein, Stan Morrison, Nick Zaccagnino, Harris Barton, Ronnie Lott, Ken Ruettgers, Wendy Spander, David Peterkofsky, Alan Isenberg, Fred Claire, David Cornwell, Brad Snyder and Adam Keefe.

TABLE OF CONTENTS

Part One

THE FUNDAMENTALS

*You had better learn how to play the game,
and I don't mean just the game of football.*
—Maxwell in the movie *North Dallas Forty*

A NOTE FROM THE AUTHOR

Sports is big-time entertainment. Games are consistently among the highest-rated television programs (the Super Bowl being *the* highest). Sports is the original reality television, with the timing of games determined by TV schedules, which in turn determine the schedule of fans' lives.

Athletes hang out with entertainers; entertainers hang out with athletes. (In fact, entertainers and athletes face similar challenges; entertainers can also apply the ideas in this book to be successful "Money Players.") Athletes become commercial pitchmen, guest stars, even actors. Corporate America wants to be identified with sports—especially with winning teams and winning athletes—because the passion they engender leads to revenue and profit.

With sports a key component of the entertainment and corporate market-places, the financial opportunities for professional athletes today are far greater than ever before. *Money Players* is about maximizing those opportunities through understanding the fundamental elements of the business of sports, including the draft, agents, players associations, owners, fans, the media, spending, saving, investing and preparing for a post-playing career. *Money Players* shows you how to apply your competitiveness to success in business as well as in sports.

I enjoy helping athletes make sense of the contradictory worlds they inhabit. In 2000, I co-authored *The Student-Athlete Survival Guide*, a book to help athletes make the transition from high school to college. For the fortunate few who have the ability to play professional sports, *Money Players* is the next step.

I wrote *Money Players* to help professional athletes, and their families and trusted advisers, deal with the social and financial aspects of a successful pro career and to sort through the often conflicting information coming from coaches, media, agents, friends and sometimes even family.

The expectations and pressures on professional athletes are enormous and mounting. Owners pay the general managers, coaches, players and even equipment managers to compete against other franchises. Our sports-crazed culture may define winning a championship as the only truly worthy outcome.

As anyone who has worked at minimum wage knows, an employer pays you to do a job. Make a mistake flipping burgers at $6.50 an hour and you might be calmly taught how to do it right. At $2 million, $3M, $10M per year, employers tend to be more impatient about getting results. *Money Players* is about improving the outcomes of the decisions you make, in and out of the athletic arena.

Professional athletes are among the most fortunate members of society, but they are also among the most vulnerable. Shady operators, ranging from outright con artists to those pitching questionable investments view professional sports as a place from which to pluck large sums of money out of the hands of young, financially inexperienced people. And while reading a book on the business of being a professional does not guarantee success, it can absolutely show you the way.

Good luck as a professional athlete—and a clutch "Money Player."

Marc Isenberg
Santa Monica, California
September 2007

PREGAME

By Ryan Nece

It is a privilege to write the "Pregame" for this book. Not only did my father, Ronnie Lott, write the "Pregame" message for Marc's first book, *The Student-Athlete Survival Guide*, but I think it is vital for pro athletes to understand the business they're in, and *Money Players* is a valuable guide to the business of professional sports.

The world of professional sports can seem confusing, particularly if you don't know what to expect going in. In reality, it's not all that complicated. It's a business. We play for the love of the game, but at the end of the day it's a job. Performers get paid. Non-performers get cut. There are ups and downs. Those who last in pro sports are able to block out the distractions, the politics and the inevitable frustrations. They show up every day ready to work.

I am incredibly fortunate to have a father who played in the NFL. My father really believes in passing the torch to younger players. He has a wealth of experience which I have benefited from, from playing in the NFL to finances to life in general. My father has been (and still is) a great role model for me, as are many of his 49er teammates, including Joe Montana, Jerry Rice, and Harris Barton. Being able to observe how these guys approached the game, how they practiced and prepared, really helped me as I entered the league.

I thought I would share a few ideas that have helped me succeed as a professional athlete:

1. Keep it simple/focus
So many things can complicate the lives of professional athletes: contracts, business relationships, off-the-field responsibilities, money, friends, family and on and on. The less these issues distract you from your sport, the better off you will be. I try to take care of my non-football affairs during the off-season and on days off.

2. Be a professional
College is supposed to prepare you for the real world. It's an opportunity to be out on your own and to take responsibility. At the same time, many college athletic departments cater to athletes, pretty much taking care of everything for them. It's not like that at the next level. Management cares only about whether you can produce as an athlete (and that you don't embarrass the franchise by what you do in your personal life). If you don't produce, they'll bring in someone who can. There are many factors that you cannot totally control, particularly injuries. But you can work hard, you can be a good teammate, and you can be a responsible adult.

3. Live below your means

When my football career ends, I want some financial rewards to show for my efforts. I think about my life after football, when I have a wife and kids. I want to be able to take care of them. I certainly don't want to look back with regret that I wasted money on extravagant things that don't enrich my life. I have a great, comfortable lifestyle. Definitely not worthy of an *MTV Cribs* feature, but that's fine by me. My rookie year in 2001, I rented *a bedroom*, not an apartment. I also drove a burnt-orange Lincoln Continental handed down from my grandmother. Keep in mind I was an undrafted free agent. I had enough pressure to just stay employed. While I spend more today, I still live modestly.

This book goes into detail about how to select the right people to work with. Don't simply accept what everyone tells you at face value. Ask tough questions. Demand answers. Great advice can be hard to find, but it's far easier to read it in a book than learn things the hard way, as many athletes have.

Reading *Money Players* is a great opportunity to learn from those who have walked in footsteps you want to follow. Good luck.

Ryan Nece is a linebacker for the NFL's Tampa Bay Buccaneers. He graduated from UCLA in 2001 with a degree in economics. He founded the Ryan Nece Foundation and co-founded the Good Samaritan Program.

DO YOU EVER GET THE FEELING
YOU'RE BEING WATCHED?

TAKE CARE OF BUSINESS...EVERY DAY

I am not a businessman/I am a business, man.
—Jay-Z lyric

Chapter highlights

- Everything important in this book is mentioned in this chapter.
- Be able to afford to spend more money every year of your life.
- You only get one shot...if you're ridiculously good and extremely lucky. Don't blow this opportunity.

You've heard a thousand times how few athletes make it to professional sports. As the NCAA announces endlessly, "There are 380,000 student-athletes and just about every one of them will go pro in something other than sports."

Congratulations! You beat the almost insurmountable odds. You have the opportunity to play the sport you love, live well, help out your family if they need it and, at the same time, build a financial foundation for the rest of your life.

However, your effort must continue on at least three fronts:

1. Athletic: To maximize the length and quality of your pro career, you have to work even harder at perfecting your skills, conditioning, studying the game, getting good nutrition and rest.

2. Social: The pressures on pro athletes are enormous. To survive and flourish requires working on keeping or building good relationships with teammates, coaches, management, media, fans, family and friends.

3. Financial: You will make a lot of money. What you will end up with at the end of your pro career depends on how much you save and how wisely you invest. Some athletes finish their playing days broke or in debt; others with enough to live well off their investments and work only if they want to.

The career window for a professional athlete is short. Every moment counts. Every good move and every mistake is magnified. Whatever you can do to maximize the length of your pro career as well as the salary you earn (and invest) will pay huge dividends for the rest of your life.

Most young people make financial mistakes. They don't save enough, or they pile up credit-card debt. They accept bad financial advice, or pay high fees for questionable or even incompetent services. Those who become successful realize their mistakes, correct them and move on. At the start of their careers, most new professionals' incomes are low, so their lessons are relatively inexpensive.

Professional athletes often do not enjoy the luxury of time to correct mistakes. The average pro career in a number of sports lasts only four years. In all too many cases, those are the top earnings years of an athlete's life. Playing catch-up is not an optimum strategy in sports, finance or life. The game often ends before early misplays can be overcome.

Build a team of professional advisers

One critical part of your success is building a great team of professional advisers who collaborate for your benefit. There are a lot of agents, business managers, lawyers, accountants, financial advisers, insurance brokers, real estate agents and other providers of professional services out there. The best are people of great integrity, experience and expertise who educate as well as serve their clients. The worst are crooks. In between are those of average competence who are mainly honest but perhaps cut a corner here or there. This book shows you how to build a team of excellent advisers.

Master the fundamentals...of business

Most of the specifics and examples in this book involve the NBA, NFL, NHL and MLB. Information about additional professional sports leagues, including the WNBA, MLS and AFL, are in the book's appendices. The issues facing pro athletes in individual sports are more similar than different. Two of the major differences in golf and tennis are that earnings from playing are based on performance and there are no unions or collective bargaining agreements. The situation of many pro athletes might be summed up this way: You suddenly have more money and fame than you did before, and despite being young and inexperienced, you have to make decisions that will affect you and your family (present and future) for the rest of your life.

Succeeding in the business of pro sports is a lot like succeeding as an athlete. In your sport, you have to master the fundamentals to perform consistently at a high level. This book is your guide to the fundamentals of business. When you began your college athletic career, you likely experienced anxiety and confusion: the players were better than high school, the game was much faster, the plays more complex. For some the transition came easy, for others it took longer and contained more setbacks. But as a serious pro prospect, you mastered the college game or the minor leagues. *Money Players* helps you master the business side of the pro game.

For the love of sport or money?

Sports is a business—a multi-billion dollar business. But athletes who play at the highest levels are driven primarily by love for the game rather than by money.

Steve Young, Pro Football Hall of Fame quarterback and lawyer, failed to deposit several paychecks. He almost felt he didn't deserve the money because of his team's poor performance. Around tax time, the 49ers' accountants couldn't reconcile the books. When they finally solved the mystery, team president Carmen Policy told Steve to cash the checks. Steve was attending law school in Utah during the off-season. He had to call a teammate in San Francisco to retrieve the checks from the glove compartment of his car.

In Michael Jordan's last two seasons playing for the Chicago Bulls, he made more than $30 million per season. Growing up in a Chicago suburb, I worked out at the same health club where the Bulls practiced. (Yes, there was a time when NBA teams did not have multi-million-dollar private practice facilities, fly on chartered jets or stay in five-star hotels.) Watching Michael in practice impressed me even more than seeing him play before sellout crowds of 17,317 at the old Chicago Stadium. He practiced just as hard against second- and third-string teammates as he played against the NBA's best. Passion for the game—not money—drove him to succeed. Of course he did—and still does —make mad money.

Control what you can

Michael Jordan understood that his offensive performance would vary. Sometimes his shot wasn't falling. Sometimes defenders played him tight. And sometimes the ball just didn't bounce his way. He viewed his defense, however, as a constant: Because he controlled his effort, Michael felt he should never have a bad night defensively. Ever.

If you have pro ability, focus on what you can do to enhance your athletic performance and get the most from your sports career, the way Michael Jordan focused on defensive effort.

This book concentrates on the areas you can control:

Character

Owners, GMs and coaches want players who can help them win. Sometimes they'll put up with less-than-model citizens—but tolerance for bad apples appears to be decreasing, even for superstars. There's a premium on "character guys"—professional athletes who can be relied on to say and do the right things. And it's these character guys who most often go on to rewarding careers as coaches, announcers and leaders in other fields.

Physical fitness and health

Take care of your body. An overweight Babe Ruth stayed up until all hours drinking and still hit 60 home runs in one season and a then-record 714 in his career. But there was only one Babe Ruth. It's a different game today: players work out year-round and endure hours and hours of daily physical therapy. Many even hire personal trainers and chefs, all to get the slightest edge.

Business and finance

Build a team of accountable experts and become knowledgeable enough to ensure that they are working in the right direction for you. Invest wisely, spend wisely and finish your playing days with a strong financial foundation for the rest of your life.

Be skeptical

Being skeptical doesn't mean you have to be distrustful. Just don't blindly trust people without taking steps to ensure that you're not being lied to or scammed. And be equally careful about advice from people who mean well, such as relatives, friends and teammates, but who may themselves be victims of misinformation or scams—or just have inadequate knowledge or poor judgment.

Think long term

Every decision you make has consequences. The results of some decisions become apparent immediately. With others it take years, even decades, before we know whether they were the right decisions.

Part Two

JOURNEY TO THE PROMISED LAND

COLLEGE RULES!

*As soon as you give a player money, you have corrupted
the relationship…it's [now] a creditor-debtor relationship.*
—Richard Woods, sports agent

There's a 100% chance you'll be offered money.
—Tim McGee, former NFL player

Chapter highlights

- Taking money or gifts from agents is a bad move.
- As a college athlete your eligibility is your most valuable asset. Protect it.
- Follow NCAA rules, even if you don't think they are fair.
- The UAAA and SPARTA elevate violations of NCAA rules to a crime.

Professional sports leagues offer rookie-orientation programs designed to help athletes handle their newfound income and the media, fans, agents and potentially disruptive outside influences. Unfortunately, as one director of player programs put it, the excitement of the first few days of a pro sports career "is not a teachable moment" for many players. Top athletes need to start learning the fundamentals of being a professional while they are still in college, if not earlier.

Dumb is not an option

You've no doubt heard this warning from you family, your coach, the NCAA and the media: "You need an education to fall back on in case you don't make it as a pro." True, but if you do become a professional athlete, you *really* need an education to deal effectively with the business aspects and to protect yourself from the questionable characters that flock to money. Even more than the subject matter of college courses, you need the skills of study and analysis developed by doing college-level work.

Agents, many; clients, few

Chapter 5 details the role of agents. Bottom line: Agents can—and typically do—provide important services for professional athletes, primarily through negotiating contracts.

Unfortunately, too many agents and would-be agents are chasing too few clients. The prizes are big: percentages of multimillion-dollar salaries and endorsement contracts. It's hard to know which athletes will succeed, so agents try to develop ties with as many pro prospects as possible. Less scrupulous agents try to buy athletes' friendship, even at the cost of endangering their NCAA eligibility, with parties, cars, cash, hotel rooms, air fares—whatever will make players feel obligated to sign with them.

Getting paid for finding gold

The old prospector in *Treasure of the Sierra Madre*, a classic movie starring Humphrey Bogart, says, "A thousand men, say, go searchin' for gold. After six months, one of them's lucky. One out of a thousand. His find represents not only his own labor, but that of nine hundred and ninety-nine others to boot...An ounce of gold, mister, is worth what it is because of the human labor that went into the finding and the getting of it."

Similarly, an agent who succeeds in signing a pro athlete gets paid for the work of all those who don't succeed. You want your advisers taking care of your business affairs, not spending the majority of their time recruiting new clients and re-recruiting existing ones.

NCAA rules on agents

The NCAA has strict rules regarding relationships between college athletes, sports agents and professional sports teams. Penalties can be severe, up to total loss of eligibility. The current rules on agents, amateurism and extra benefits are published annually in the *NCAA Division 1 Manual* and posted online at www.ncaa.org. The NCAA office of Agent, Gambling and Amateurism has also posted memorandums for college football, baseball and basketball athletes considering a pro career (Follow: NCAA.org > Legislation & Governance > Agents & Amateurism > Agent Information for Student-Athletes). Although the language can be confusing, it pays to familiarize yourself with these rules. Situations may arise where knowing these rules could save your sports career. When you're faced with an issue that may impact your eligibility, consult your school's compliance officer and/or contact the NCAA for information you can rely on. Otherwise, you run the risk of misinterpreting the rules, which is a poor defense if you are caught.

Many colleges have added their own restrictions on when and how agents can approach you. Some require that agents first register with the athletic department, or even attempt to approach you only through the athletic department. Or that agents stay away except at specified times, for example on "Agent Day." Most of these rules do not explicitly prohibit you from contacting an agent.

Here is a short, plain-English summary of the NCAA rules regarding agents, amateurism and eligibility.

Five Don'ts and One Do

> *Don't* take money or other benefits (including free transportation) from an agent (or anyone else who is giving them to you because you are an athlete).
> *Don't* agree to be represented by an agent, either orally or in writing.
> *Don't* allow an agent to act as an agent on your behalf.
> *Don't* sign with a professional sports team or play on a team that compensates players, even if you play for free.
> *Don't* accept any payment based on your or your team's performance.

> *Do* get advice from an agent, lawyer or anyone else—as long as he or she does not promote your athletic skills to pro teams or negotiate a contract between you and a team. Just beware of anything that even looks like representation by an agent.

Agents with mob muscle

Lloyd Bloom and Norby Walters were the principals in the biggest agent scandal in college sports history. (Of course, to qualify as a scandal it had to come to light, so there may well have been larger, more successful operations.) Bloom and Walters paid a total of $800,000 to more than 30 college athletes. In 1987, they gave money to at least five first-round NFL draft picks. When these athletes selected others to be their agents, Walters filed beach of contract suits against them and ratted them out to the media.

"I'm suing these players because they have wronged me," Walters said. "I've taken care of their mommies and their daddies and their babies and their cars. They are the immoral ones. They took the money from the schools. They took the money from their alumni. They signed a contract with me…I will continue to sue each and every businessman who goes into business with me and breaks the contract."

Michael Franzese, a former Mafia capo in the Colombo crime family who served three years in prison for racketeering, invested in Walters and Bloom's agency. His outfit reportedly provided muscle to intimidate athletes and competing agents. One female competitor was mugged at knifepoint.

Bloom and Walters went to prison. Bloom was later murdered. Today Franzese is an NCAA-approved speaker on gambling and organized crime.

Blame agents

The NCAA and its members would prefer that talented athletes complete their college eligibility. From their point of view, the departure of players who win big games and draw big crowds—and who also leave without their degrees—is a loss. Their return on investment in recruiting and training is reduced by one, two or even three seasons. Of course, from the point of view of an athlete who makes a successful transition, jumping to the pros is a win. It's self-realization and financial return on an investment of years of hard work and sacrifice.

Some associated with college athletics blame "agents of corruption" for jeopardizing the eligibility of unsuspecting college athletes. They view agents with disdain and do their best to banish agents from locker rooms and even from campuses. If they catch an athlete taking money from an agent, they deliver swift and severe punishment.

Unfortunately, this strategy does not work. If the NCAA and its schools could police every locker room, dorm, hotel lobby and athletes' hangout, they would discover an underground system of "runners," people who develop relationships with athletes on behalf of agents and financial advisers without necessarily identifying whom they represent. They would further discover that this network is self-replenishing: Catch a runner and two more take his place. As long as big bucks flow to those who represent and advise pro athletes, agents and their runners will be out to "befriend" potential pros.

There's nothing wrong with agents openly making appropriate inquiries, just as there is nothing wrong with college coaches contacting high school recruits within NCAA rules. The problem is when agents endanger an athlete's eligibility by not following the rules or distract an athlete from focusing on improving his skills.

The NCAA has developed a three-pronged approach to deal with the issue of agents on campus:

1. Education
The NCAA and schools try to educate college athletes about the dangers of associating with agents. The NCAA distributes *A Career In Professional Athletics*, a booklet that provides information about the business of pro sports, but also provides the NCAA do's and don'ts when it comes to agents.

2. Lobbying
The NCAA and its members have successfully lobbied states to pass laws requiring agents to register with the state and that criminalize agent activities that violate NCAA rules. The laws also criminalize certain behavior by student-athletes, such as signing with an agent and not revealing it to the school. As of August 2007, the Uniform Amateur Agent Act (UAAA) had been passed in 36 states, plus the District of Columbia and U.S. Virgin Islands. The NCAA lobbied for a similar law at the federal level. In 2004, President Bush signed The Sports Agent and Responsibility Trust Act (SPARTA) into law. SPARTA is the federal equivalent of UAAA minus certain requirements, such as agent registration.

3. For championships, elevating rule breaking to criminal activity
If you're not yet convinced of the compelling necessity to follow NCAA rules, this is the clincher. The NCAA currently requires student-athletes participating in NCAA Championships in D-1 basketball (men's and women's) and D-1 baseball and Division 1-A football to sign an affidavit that they have not violated NCAA rules. An affidavit is a legal document. If an athlete provides a false statement in the affidavit—a likely scenario for someone who already

violated an NCAA rule, but does not want to forfeit his eligibility—this document provides schools with legal remedies. In concert with the above-stated laws, schools could use this document to bolster a civil case against an athlete accused of violating any NCAA rules, such as those regarding agents, amateurism and gambling.

Look ma, no agents

There are some agents who might try to get around the rules by giving gifts to your parents. Doesn't work. The NCAA holds athletes responsible if family members or friends accept offerings from agents. You could lose your eligibility if an agent treats your parents to dinner. It is your responsibility to educate your family members and friends about the NCAA rules. Primarily, you want to explain how their actions could affect your eligibility. Less obvious, perhaps, is that you don't want friends and family making promises on your behalf, especially if you have not authorized them to do so.

"The athletes stuck me with the check"

Mel Levine kept meticulous records of money he paid to NCAA athletes. Several did not sign with him, and Levine sued. In his 1993 book, *Life in the Trash Line: Cash, Cars and Corruption, a Sports Agent's True Story*, Levine writes, "In time I was to represent the cream of the National Football League crop, including talents like Michael Irvin, Bennie and Brian Blades, Brett Perriman, Jon Geisler and Duriel Harris. At the same time I was setting up future clients, college recruits who would break NCAA eligibility requirements and sign with me in exchange for cars and cash. Unfortunately, time and time again they would stay true to form and stick me with the check." About one athlete, whom he says took $25,000 from him, Levine writes, "It gives me great satisfaction to expose [guys like him to] the world, egomaniacs eager to take and never pay back. Portrayed as innocent pawns in the big game of NFL owners and agents, players are an integral part of the disease."

Hands down: the best advice

What if there were no prohibitions against taking money, gifts or favors from agents? Would you grab everything you could?

Let's back up a step. At various times you've probably been offered some type of "hook up," something apparently for nothing. A favor here, a free lunch there. Such generosity may come your way because you're an athlete—or not. Favors are used throughout our society to build relationships.

As an elite athlete, you have likely been offered freebies or special deals that go beyond the norm. Shoes, clothes, equipment, meals, entertainment, travel, cushy or no-show summer jobs, cars, apartments and money are among the enticing goodies made available to selected athletes. These offers sometimes start as early as the fifth grade. What could be more natural than to put your hand out and say, "Yes, thanks"? But once you've started along the path of easy acceptance, it's hard to change course as the gifts become bigger and better. Then, you've put yourself in a place where it's hard to make an independent decision. You may feel obligated to select an agent who may not be competent and who is definitely not ethical. **If you do end up hiring him, you will pay for all those gifts you received many times over, and your money will be used to dangle similar bait in front of other prospects.**

Instead of loans disguised as favors from agents who want to represent you, take a proactive approach. Chapter 5 recommends setting up criteria that candidates must meet before you even interview them.

Reason #968 to follow NCAA extra benefits rules

Extra-benefit cases involving NCAA athletes often come to light when individuals (typically wannabe agents) claim they are owed money by college athletes. Convicted criminals Michael Michaels and Lloyd Lake alleged that Reggie Bush's parents lived rent-free in a house owned by Michaels while Bush was playing at USC. The duo claimed they provided $100,000 cash and other benefits to the Bush family and invested another $200,000 to start a sports agency that would represent Bush when he turned pro. Bush signed with another agent and another marketing firm. Michaels and Lake demanded Bush pay them $3.2 million to settle their "economic loss." Their demand letter included a not-so-subtle hint that the NCAA and the media would have an interest in this matter. It read in part, "Please advise if it is your intention to involve the University [of Southern California] in these settlement negotiations. We would not object to their participation as we understand their wanting to be involved due to the fact this matter was ongoing during their championship season of 2004 as well as the entire season of 2005, and any lawsuit filed might have an adverse effect on them." Can you say extortion? According to newspaper reports, the dispute between Bush and Michaels was settled out of court in April 2007.

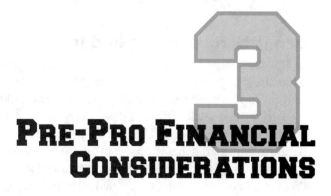

Pre-Pro Financial Considerations

Too many people spend money they haven't earned, to buy things they don't want, to impress people they don't like.
—Will Smith, actor

Chapter highlights

- Avoid credit card debt.
- Although the chance of a career-ending injury is remote, disability insurance for college athletes may be appropriate for sure-fire pro prospects, if only for peace of mind.

As an amateur athlete, you're not being paid to play. Yet, your performance will have an enormous impact on your financial future. If you're like most pro prospects, when you read the last sentence, you thought of athletic performance. And of course that's true. But your performance *off* the field or court may have as much—or more—effect on whether you end up wealthy or broke. Whether you succeed in the business of pro sports depends largely on

➤ The people you surround yourself with.
➤ The decisions you make (and the process you use for making decisions).
➤ How you spend your money.
➤ Debt you may acquire.

College is an investment in your future. Hard work in your sport hopefully pays future dividends. Similarly, hard work on the variables listed above can lead to maximizing the return on what you earn as an athlete.

Earn it before you spend it

The U.S. tax system rewards saving. Yet in 2006 the savings rate was *minus* 1%, meaning people on the average spent 1% more than they earned. This rate is the lowest since the Great Depression of the 1930s. Consumer debt is also on the rise. According to a 2004 study by the American Council on Education, more than 60% of bachelor's degree recipients graduated with federal student-loan debt. The median amount borrowed was $14,671 at public institutions and $17,125 at private institutions. In addition, more than 48% of recent college graduates carried over monthly credit card balances; the median balance owed was $1,579.

If you received an athletic scholarship, you should be in much better financial shape than students who had to pay for their education. Since the average starting salary of professional athletes is far above that of college graduates in other professions, you are in an enviable situation.

But the ready availability of credit cards makes it easy to spend irresponsibly, especially for those who don't understand the cost of buying on credit. As an aspiring professional athlete, you are even more vulnerable, because your current spending habits may be influenced by what you think you will earn in the future.

Instant bad decision

For legitimate pro prospects instant gratification can be a matter of saying "yes." The standard advice is, "Don't violate NCAA rules by accepting extra benefits." But the decision is often more complicated than, "Just say no."

For some college athletes, the rationalization might go something like…

The NCAA's $6-billion deal with CBS.
My coach makes $2 million per year.
The school sells $100 jerseys with my name/number.
College sports is a full-time, year-round job.
Everybody is getting rich in the business of big-time college sports, but me. I'm poor.

In reality, tough luck. If you decide to play NCAA sports, you must agree to play by its rules. If you believe the rules are unfair, you have every right to voice your concerns; even fight for change. But cheating (even if you don't get caught) is a short-sighted decision that comes with significant risk to your eligibility as well as your ability to make independent, sound business decisions.

Between amateur and pro

After you have exhausted your eligibility (or otherwise declared for the draft), agents, financial advisers and others who are courting you may entice you with immediate sums of money, often in the form of a letter of credit. Obviously, cash in hand can be compelling. But hold on, you're almost there.

You will need some money to live and train. It has become common practice for agents to foot the bill, particularly for projected top picks. There's nothing wrong with improving your lifestyle beyond how you lived as an amateur athlete. Just go slow. Your focus should be on preparing for the draft—and little else.

Depending on where you're projected to go in the draft, you can access hundreds of thousands of dollars of credit, if not more. But it's not free money. It's like a giant credit card. You are obligated to pay it back whether you are drafted or not, and the interest rates tend to be high.

Every year a few draft prospects start spending as if they were certain of being drafted in the first round, including buying expensive cars and throwing open-bar draft parties. Veteran pros describe pre-contract big spending as a typical "rookie mistake." It's silly to spend money you don't have on non-essentials. If you are in a position to generate some marketing deals before the draft, do that. It's a good way to start earning money. If you need to borrow, borrow sparingly.

Consider insurance against injury

Elite college athletes who choose to stay in school for an additional year or two rather than go pro can purchase insurance policies that pay off in the event of a career-ending injury or illness. Policies are available through the NCAA in collaboration with insurance company HCC Specialty Underwriters, and through independent insurance agents using Lloyd's of London as the insurance provider. In either case, the athlete can obtain a loan from a bank to pay the insurance premium. Athletes who borrow money to buy these policies must pay back the money, with interest, regardless of whether they sign a pro contract. Details of the NCAA's Exceptional Student-Athlete Disability Insurance program are available on the NCAA's Web site, www.ncaa.org.

In order to participate in the NCAA-sponsored program, NCAA athletes must be projected to be drafted in the early rounds (in football in the first three rounds). Private insurers use similar guidelines in determining whether to offer this type of policy, as do banks in deciding whether to loan athletes money to pay the premiums.

These insurance policies pay out only in the event of an injury or illness that ends your pro career before it starts. They do not pay if you are able to play despite an injury or illness that diminishes your skills, lowers your position in the draft, or causes loss of a pro season while recovering from an injury. As a result of advances in medical treatment, career-ending injuries are rare. For example, most anterior cruciate ligament (ACL) injuries now keep a player out for six to eight months, but rarely end careers.

An athlete disability policy from Lloyd's of London states, "Total disability or totally disabled means solely and directly as a result of injury or sickness the insured is certified by a physician as being wholly and continuously prevented from engaging in the Occupation/Sport stated."

Most policies are written for one year and include 24-hour coverage, usually excluding accidents caused under the influence of drugs and alcohol, flying as a pilot and self-inflicted injury.

Even in the event of a career-ending injury, if the insurer finds (through drug testing) that the athlete has been using illegal substances or perfor-mance-enhancing drugs such as steroids, the payout could be contested. The NCAA declined to tell me how many claims have paid out, but stated to the press that "less than a half dozen claims have been made." Of course, there's a big difference between filing a claim and collecting. In the history of the NCAA program, which was initiated in 1990, a media search revealed only one instance of a payout: In 1998, Ed Chester, a Florida defensive tackle who severely injured his knee, collected $1 million on a policy that cost him $8,000.

There are several differences between the NCAA-HCC policy and the Lloyd's of London policy, including the following: Lloyd's of London does not limit the amount of insurance an athlete can buy. NCAA policies place upper limits on the amount, as follows:

Football: $3 million
Men's basketball: $4.4 million
Ice hockey: $1.2 million
Baseball: $1.5 million
Women's basketball: $250,000

In the event of a career-ending injury, Lloyd's of London pays the entire award in one payment; NCAA-HCC pays in five equal payments over a period of 30 months. If you're a bona-fide pro prospect forgoing millions of dollars in order to stay in school, it might make sense to purchase disability insurance, although I suspect the insurance companies charge too much relative to the actual likelihood of a career-ending injury. You do have to pay back whatever you borrow to buy this insurance, but that amount is a small percentage relative to what you will make as a pro athlete—and it will give you peace of mind.

I'D SAY HE TURNED PRO TOO EARLY.

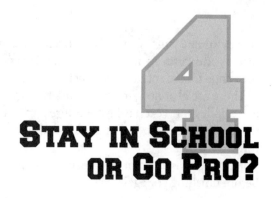

STAY IN SCHOOL OR GO PRO?

*The goal should not be to get to the NBA. It should be to **stay** in the NBA.*
—Jerry West, former superstar guard, Los Angeles Lakers, longtime
NBA general manager, and the silhouette in the NBA logo

Why is it nobody asks a [college athlete] if he's staying?
It's always "Are you going?"
—Al Groh, head football coach, University of Virginia

Chapter highlights
- Jerry West's quote above sums it all up.
- College isn't for everyone.
- If in doubt, wait it out.

The case for jumping to the pros

Some college coaches have tremendous resumes when it comes to preparing players for professional sports. Obviously, your coach wants to improve your skills. However, a college coach's job is to win games, not to help you go pro. No matter what you were promised while you were being recruited, your coach knows his job depends on winning. If winning requires, for example, that you play a different position than the one that gives you your best shot at the pro draft, that's where you'll play. The hope is that your college team's success will enhance your pro chances, but it's not automatic. Evaluate how much the coach is helping you by helping himself and his program.

Also, evaluate your competition. Even as teenagers, elite European basketball players and Latin American baseball players often train 8 to 10 hours a day. As a college student, it's virtually impossible to do that.

There are also non-sports factors that weigh on your decision to stay or leave college. If you have little interest in being a student and are just trying to stay eligible to play, that could (and perhaps should) make you lean toward leaving.

What combination of circumstances might make it reasonable to turn pro before finishing college?

- An objective estimate of your value as a pro
- High level of athletic development
- Maturity to cope with life in the pros

Let's look at each of these points.

An objective estimate of your value as a pro

If you are going to be a first-round pick in most professional leagues, you will sign a contract that will guarantee you millions of dollars. Let's face it, that much money is hard to pass up. And you can always work on your college degree during the off-season.

If you play an individual sport such as golf or tennis, there is no draft and no contract. You become a pro by qualifying and entering pro competitions. Your earnings are based on how high you place in those competitions. Just as for a team sport player, it comes down to analyzing your abilities. There's no denying Tiger Woods made the right decision in leaving Stanford after his sophomore year. But there are plenty of names that escape me (and everyone else) who did the same thing with different results.

Turning pro before your eligibility expires is always a gamble. How can an athlete make the most objective estimate? By using the same techniques that work in the college recruiting process:

- Ask questions.
- Listen.
- Don't rely on the advice of only one person.
- Understand the financial interests of everyone involved.
- Take time to think and rethink; don't decide under pressure.
- Check that your decision conforms to your basic values.

High level of athletic development

A pro team may draft you high because of your potential, but they will not wait indefinitely for you to live up to it. They want to see a return on their investment. Some college players have reached the point where they need to practice and play at the pro level to improve. But if your skills or body need more time to develop to reach that point, staying in college will increase your chances of success in the pros. Working with your college coach for an additional year or two can make a big difference. Think it through. Focus on making yourself the best athlete you can become. The money will follow.

Maturity to cope with life in the pros

Professional sports is much tougher than even big-time college sports (and in a different universe from high school sports). Everything becomes magnified: the media, the fans and sports-talk radio view professional sports as fair game. If your game falls slightly below the unreasonable expectations, you become an easy target for brutal criticism. Understand how rigorous this can be and ask yourself if you're ready. Life in the pros is not revealed on television. It has nothing to do with what we see on *Inside Stuff* or *Cribs*. The "NBA is fantastic"—for the fans. And it is glamorous to play in professional sports. But it's also a grind: the grueling schedule, the intense pain, the constant travel, the hotels, the media, the fans. You might decide another year or two of emotional and intellectual maturity would help you succeed as a pro even if, as an athlete, you are ready now.

> *I am not saying I'm ready for the NBA now, but I am ready to get drafted.* —Ndudi Ebi, who was a first round pick, but has played in only 19 games in his NBA career

The case for staying in college

Many athletes are so focused on getting into professional sports that they never think beyond that. As Jerry West said, the goal shouldn't be just to *get to the pros*, it should be to *stay in the pros*. Do you want to be a first-round pick, sign a rookie contract and then be out of the League after a couple of seasons? Or is your goal to have a 10-year career?

College prepares you for a job, whether in business, medicine, law or sports. For most athletes, it is the place to hone the skills needed to succeed as a pro. Playing three or four years of ACC or Pac-10 basketball, for example, is great training, even if your alternative is to be a lottery pick straight out of high school or after a year of college.

The NBA picked players out of high school—Kevin Garnett, Kobe Bryant, Tracy McGrady, Jermaine O'Neal, LeBron James, Martell Webster—because of their enormous potential. (The NBA now requires players to be 19 years old and one year past high school graduation to be eligible for the draft.) The same goes for many athletes who left college after one or two years. College graduates Grant Hill, Tim Duncan, and Shane Battier were a different story. Having moved beyond potential, they showed up on day one prepared for the rigors of the NBA. One promising player who honed his skills in college for three years: Michael Jordan.

You may decide that you want to stay in college no matter how many millions pro sports may offer. The reasons could include:

- Getting a degree to satisfy you and/or your parents.
- Enjoyment of college sports.
- A goal such as a championship or individual award.
- Improving your athletic skills.
- Developing physically.
- Maturing emotionally.

Go pro, young man

The sheer number of players leaving early, particularly in basketball, proves that many are making a bad decision (45 underclassmen declared for the 2007 NBA Draft.) At the same time there are legitimate reasons for leaving: risk of injury, money, and disdain for school. While there are coaches who probably would prefer their players to stay all four years, that's not realistic—or fair. Reputable college coaches generally shoot straight with athletes when it comes to the heady decision to turn pro or stay in school. Today's reality is that most college basketball superstars don't stay in school four years.

There is no "one size fits all" advice when it comes to the final decision. Former UNC coach Dean Smith would tell players: "We have one rule here: We do what's best for the player out of season and what's best for the team in season." Coach Smith would generally advise players projected to be top 10 picks to come out early primarily because they could secure their financial future. If a player is projected to be an NBA lottery pick (among the first 12 selected), most coaches (and unbiased experts) will support a player's decision to turn pro. Memphis basketball coach John Calipari famously tore up Dejuan Wagner's scholarship immediately after his freshman year to "make sure he understood he wasn't coming back." Wagner was the sixth pick in the 2002 NBA Draft, but lasted only three years due to medical problems. Said Calipari: "Now you might say [Wagner's] out of the league, but he made $15 million."

Declaring early for NFL Draft

The key question for athletes who might consider turning pro early is, "Is there any upside in my development as a pro prospect?" Take a projected first or second round NFL pick (based on NFL evaluation, not just a random poll of agents and draft experts). Will another year of seasoning improve his draft stock enough to compensate for all the risks, including not just injury, but also the real possibility that the player may not be selected in the following year's draft? On the other hand, many players can benefit from another year of college and can, in fact, improve their draft status. In football, where the risks are significant, if there is little upside, then the risk of injury and skill diminishment (real or perceived) dictates that the player turns pro.
—Jack Mills, football agent

To go or not to go?

That is the question trying the souls of many athletes. Get the best advice you can get. Then it's your responsibility to evaluate the advice, make a decision, and live with it. Career choice is not an exact science. You will never know if you made the right decision except in hindsight and maybe not even then. You may have the physical and mental toughness to thrive in the pros at a young age. We do know that for every success story, many athletes leave school only to see their dreams of pro glory become nightmares. Pro sports isn't going anywhere. It will be around a year from now. And so will the money (probably in greater amounts). My overall advice: If in doubt, wait it out.

SELECT YOUR AGENT

A lot of players didn't have agents [in the early 1970s]. We couldn't understand why we should pay an agent a commission for not getting us the same salary we couldn't get on our own.
—Terry Bradshaw, Pro Football Hall of Fame quarterback and NFL on Fox broadcaster

Chapter highlights

- There are too many agents.
- There are good agents, despite generally negative press.
- Selecting the right agent is critical.

The real-life Jerry Maguire

Sports agents have cultivated a bigger-than-life persona. We see and hear real-life agents on TV and radio, and see movies, such as *Jerry Maguire, He Got Game, Heaven Is a Playground* and *Above the Rim*, that feature fictional agents. Becoming a sports agent is the dream job of many idealistic young students and recent grads. The reality is often far different: a tough business with ruthless competitors and sometimes dysfunctional relationships with clients.

Agents often get a bad rap. Some of the criticism is deserved; much is not. As in any profession, some agents are sleazy and unscrupulous. They endanger athletes by breaking NCAA rules and federal and state laws, and providing bad or even negligent advice. After one too many "all agents are sleazebags" articles, Michael Wright, an IMG sports agent, wrote in the *Sports Business Journal*, "I have engaged in this business for almost 20 years. The vast majority of agents I have dealt with over that time have been honorable men and women, serving the needs of their clients in an ethical manner...It is our job, however, to advise, guide, and assist our clients on the business side of sport to balance the playing field, if you will, so they are not taken advantage of."

How good agents add value

Sports agents negotiate contracts for their clients. As playing salaries have become more standardized, the value of having an agent has been called into question. However, the majority of pro athletes benefit from having an agent (or a lawyer who performs some of the same functions but is compensated differently). In addition to helping with those areas of your contract that are negotiable, a good agent can:

> Help you prepare for the draft.
> Protect you from rookie mistakes.
> Educate you about collective bargaining issues.
> In some cases, help you maximize other financial opportunities, such as endorsements.
> Refer you to other professionals, such as business managers and financial advisers (whom you should independently screen).

Your agent and your draft prospects

Just about every serious draft prospect will engage the services of a sports agent. As Jonathan Givony, founder of DraftExpress.com, explains below with reference to the NBA Draft, a knowledgeable agent becomes your draft guru. After all, this will be your first—and in most cases only—experience with the draft, so it's important to hire an agent who has the expertise to guide you through the draft process and to negotiate the best possible playing and marketing deals.

Agent as NBA draft guide

"Agents play an essential role in helping steer their clients through the often very complicated NBA draft process. Starting with knowing the timing of when to declare for the draft, gathering feedback from NBA executives on a player's draft stock, picking a suitable trainer to prepare for private workouts and (potentially) the pre-draft camp, setting up workouts and managing the 'hype' factor that can play a role in where a player is selected, and much, much more—the wrong choice at this early stage can end up delivering a serious setback that some players just can't recover from, shooting a career down before it ever gets off the ground."

—Jonathan Givony, president, DraftExpress.com

Your agent and your contract

The market for professional athletes is similar to the stock market. Salaries are based on expected future performance and what this expected production is worth in the marketplace. If a player is not a free agent, his value is limited by what his current team is willing to pay. Or, if a player is a *restricted* free agent, his value is greater, but still limited by restrictions, including the current team's right of first refusal (right to match). An *unrestricted* free agent essentially participates in a free market system, with salary determined on the open market. Teams may, however, be restricted by salary cap or luxury tax.

It is the responsibility of sports agents to understand the quick-changing economics of professional sports and get maximum value for their clients. If a player signs a bad deal, it can negatively impact not only his future, but the negotiations of other players as well.

Agent certification and regulation

In order to protect its members, PAs certify and regulate the professional conduct of agents. Leagues may require "certified contract advisers" (sports agents) to:

- Submit to background checks (to eliminate anyone who has a felony conviction)
- Pass a certification test
- Attend annual seminars
- Pay dues

Some PAs require agents to have players on active rosters as a condition of certification. The NFLPA will de-certify an agent who goes three years without having a client. Also, professional leagues will only approve player contracts negotiated by certified agents and fine teams who negotiate with an uncertified agent. Players are entitled to waive this right if they negotiate their own contract. The certification and oversight of agents does not itself guarantee that a player will receive competent representation, but it does provide some safety.

Agent fees

You want to hire the best possible agent and be charged a reasonable fee. Consider that typically the best surgeon (or the best anything) is also the most expensive. There's no right price for the wrong surgeon. There is, however, growing pressure on agents to reduce their fees. The pressure comes from competition: with too many agents chasing too few clients, some compete on price. And with lawyers charging hourly fees to negotiate contracts, an agent's percentage fee can look large by contrast. The pressure also comes from players associations and athletes, who point out that negotiating uniform playing contracts is relatively straightforward, especially NBA rookie contracts.

What agents should charge is open for debate—and negotiation. Evaluate all aspects of a potential agent, not just the fee. Some agents are willing to cut fees, particularly for high-profile players with marketing value. High-profile players add cache for the agency, and the real financial reward in representing them is in marketing deals, where an agent typically charges 10-25%.

League	No. of Certified Agents	No. of active players (approx.)	Agent fee cap
NFL	900	1440	3%
NBA	320	360	4%
MLB	300	750	None
NHL	150	750	None
WNBA	41	169	5%

As the chart shows, agent fees are not capped in hockey and baseball. The MLBPA is nothing if not consistent, stating, "Just as the Association endorses a free market system for its players in negotiating contracts with Club owners, the agent fee is negotiated freely between the player and his agent."

Flat fee versus billable hours

Some professional athletes have hired lawyers to negotiate their contracts. Instead of charging a percentage, like an agent, most lawyers bill on an hourly basis. This generally results in a lower fee. In 2000, Grant Hill, for example, signed a seven-year, $93-million contract with the NBA's Orlando Magic. Instead of paying 3% of the total contract ($2.8 million) to an agent, Hill reportedly paid the law firm of Williams and Connolly $350,000 to negotiate his deal. Lon Babby and James Tanner, lawyers at Williams and Connolly, have evolved their practice into a full-service sports agency within the law firm. They charge an hourly rate for all their services, including marketing, with fees capped at 4%. This model may not be right for every pro athlete. Everything depends on what makes the most sense, given a pro athlete's own set of circumstances.

Guarantees

Agents are not supposed to provide inducements to get prospective clients to sign, even after a player has completed his college eligibility. The reason: an agent should be selected on the basis of ability, not cash or gifts. Some agencies offer high-profile athletes "marketing guarantees." An agent guarantees that the athlete will earn a certain amount from marketing deals. If there is a shortfall, the agency must pay it out of pocket. Additionally, the agency collects commission only on revenue generated above the guarantee. These arrangements are legal and, if they are not inducements, do not violate players association regulations. Guarantees can be good for the athlete. But buyer beware: The agent with the biggest bankroll is not always the best agent.

Marketing fees

In addition to negotiating the playing contract, many sports agents also handle marketing deals for athletes. While playing contracts come under strict regulation by players associations, marketing deals are unregulated. Marketing agents typically charge 10-25%. Obviously, you want a marketing agent to have the incentive to hustle for deals. But you also want to negotiate a fair percentage based on how much value you believe your marketing agent brings to the table.

Terminating player/agent relationship

An NBA, NFL or MLB player or his agent can terminate the standard-player agent contract at any time, with or without cause. If an athlete—or even the agent—terminates a standard or uniform player contract, fees are owed to the agent for the duration of that contract. This might not seem fair, but legal precedent holds that an agent's fee is earned once the contract is negotiated, and not for any ongoing work.

Signs of a good agent	Signs of bad agent
Transparent, understandable reports	Poor, hard to follow explanations
Gets clients through referrals	Focuses too much energy on recruiting
Separates agent and investing functions	Uses one-stop shopping to control clients
Helps institute proper controls and oversight	Resists accountability procedures

Too Many Choices

Have you ever been to In-N-Out Burger? Displayed above the counter are your choices:

1. Double-Double, Cheeseburger, Hamburger
2. Fries
3. Shake (3 flavors), Beverage (8 choices).

That's it, 1-2-3. But if you went to any Jerry's Deli in Southern California, or Carnegie Deli in New York City, you're faced with the daunting task of identifying the best menu item from a newspaper-sized offering of choices. Torture. Immediately after you order, you often find yourself wishing you made a different choice. The Lesson: The more seemingly attractive choices, the harder it is to choose the best one. It's exactly the situation facing athletes who attempt to select the best agents and advisers from a crowded field. While the final decision may come down to comfort level and gut feelings, keep in mind that these are often poor indicators. Selecting the right agent takes work. You might even have to go beyond your comfort zone—and your locker room—to find the best agent.

How to select the right agent

Ideally the first agent you select will be the right agent. The key words here are "you select" the agent, rather than having the agent select you through becoming your "friend" and giving you "gifts." Finding the right agent is not easy, especially when you are relatively new to the business. To increase the chance that you make the right choice, set up a system that potential agents must follow if they want to represent you. Here are some possible criteria to include:

- ➤ Appoint an intermediary. Advise agents that instead of approaching you directly, they must contact someone you designate, such as a parent, coach or other trusted adviser.
- ➤ Consult with your college's professional sports counseling panel if your school has one and it is considered effective. These panels often include, for example, business and/or law school professors; they can be excellent sources of free, expert advise.
- ➤ Require written submissions. Advise agents that you require written materials that include the following:
  - Names of all athletes they currently represent.
  - Contact info of three current or former clients.
  - Names of all active athletes who left the agency during the past five years
  - If they have ever been sued by an athlete or reprimanded or suspended by a players association, the details.
  - If they have ever been charged criminally or otherwise disbarred or reprimanded by an oversight body (Securities & Exchange Commission) or professional organization (American Bar Association), the details of these circumstances.
  - A resumé or biography with their educational and professional background.
  - A description of how they have helped a player succeed in the draft.
  - Their policy on working with a trainer prior the draft. Can you select your own trainer?
  - A description of all the services their agency provides in-house, and which services they refer to other professionals.
  - How they work with their clients' other professional advisers (financial adviser, marketing agent, lawyer, insurance broker, etc.).
  - A description of how and how much they get paid, including all commissions, fees and expenses that you would pay for each service and that they would receive from other sources, if any, in connection with being your representative.
- ➤ Before interviewing agents, read their written submissions.
- ➤ Before interviewing a candidate, contact the three client references they provided. Explain that you are considering hiring the agent in question, and would appreciate knowing about their experience and how satisfied they are.

- Interview only those who pass the above scrutiny.
- Have your trusted adviser participate in the interview, and compare notes afterward.
- Even if you "really like" one candidate, interview the others who have passed your screening. Make a decision only after you have had some time to compare the strengths and weaknesses of the best candidates.

"Increase the chance you will get qualified representation"

There are no guarantees, but if you go through a process like the one Marc described, you are very likely to end up with an ethical, competent agent. If you select one based on gifts received and partying together, you are very likely to end up with an incompetent agent.

Don't be swayed by smooth, aggressive and often expensive sales pitches. The best agents aren't necessarily the high-profile ones on TV who are getting quoted in the media. You want skilled negotiators who understand the marketplace and pay close attention to detail.

If you don't understand the issues affecting your career, you're increasing the chances that an agent takes advantage of your inexperience. If you do your research, ask a lot of questions and are generally involved, you increase the chance that you will get qualified representation.

Once you hire an agent, you still need to stay involved. If you don't, you will have no way to know whether you are getting adequate representation.

Always remember that agents serve at your pleasure. If an agent isn't doing his job, you can terminate the relationship by sending official notification to the NBPA office.

—Adonal Foyle, NBA player

THE DRAFT IS COMING, PEOPLE! WE MUST KNOW *EVERYTHING* ABOUT THIS PROSPECT!

HOW THE DRAFT WORKS

Draft day is not the important day. It's what I do after the draft that's important.
—Joe Thomas, Wisconsin tackle, No. 3 overall pick in the 2007 NFL Draft

Chapter highlights

- The NBA and NFL offer objective evaluations of where you are likely to be selected.
- Baseball prospects have the most leverage when it comes to negotiating a professional contract.
- Skip the stuff in this chapter that does not apply to your sport's draft.

Although having a long pro career is even more significant, draft position is critical for aspiring professional athletes. Millions of dollars in guaranteed bonuses and contracts are on the line.

When a team selects a player in the draft, that team not only makes an investment via signing bonus and playing salary, but it also makes a commitment to that player. If an undrafted free agent doesn't perform, the solution is simple and inexpensive: Thank you, and here's a one-way ticket home. High draft picks enjoy at least three advantages. First, they get opportunities to play. Second, general managers and even coaches have a vested interest in seeing them succeed. Third, if they fail, they get second and even third looks from other teams.

This chapter describes how the draft works; the following chapter gives you a strategy to prepare for the draft.

Uncertainty reigns

No matter how thoroughly athletes and teams prepare, the draft remains an uncertain process. In that regard, aspiring professional athletes resemble other college graduates entering the workforce, except for the prospect of more zeroes on their paychecks.

The draft is based primarily on potential. Even general managers, who are paid to predict how well athletes will perform as pros, make embarrassing mistakes. The athlete's problem can be complicated by ego, media hype, the hopes and wishes of family and friends, and by advice from people with a financial stake in the decision.

You don't know with any degree of certainty where you'll be picked in the draft. An agent may imply that a high-level inside source with a team has told him they will "definitely select you" with their first-round selection. The truth is agents have little input about where a player is selected in the draft and, whatever they are told or not told (or want to believe, or want you to believe) may have no relationship to what actually happens on draft day.

General managers do not commit to a player before making a full evaluation at all-star games, scouting combines and through individual testing. In basketball and football, that process doesn't start for an underclassman until he applies for the draft. With the exception of athletes who are clearly the cream of the crop, all you can really get is a reasonable estimate as to where you are projected to be drafted. Unfortunately, that's not much reassurance when such a major decision is involved. A player thought to be a fourth-round pick can move himself up to a first-round pick in a short time. Just as quickly, a "sure-fire first-round pick" can plummet to the second round, or even right out of the draft.

Here is a brief outline of how each league's draft works.

MLB Draft

Number of rounds: Approximately 50 (1,500 draftees)
When: June

The baseball draft is the most complex. In baseball there is no such thing as "declaring for the draft." Prospects are eligible to be drafted by major league teams at several stages, depending on age, collegiate affiliation and nationality. Who is eligible?

- U.S. players, if they have graduated from high school and have not yet attended any college or junior college;
- U.S. players from four-year colleges who have either completed their junior or senior years or are at least 21 years old; junior college players, regardless of how many years of school they have completed; and
- U.S. players who are at least 21 years old.

Only residents of Canada, the United States, Puerto Rico and other U.S. territories are eligible for the draft.

Interestingly, foreign players (such as the large contingent from the Dominican Republic), while not eligible to be drafted, can be signed by major league teams at age 16!

If a team offers a contract that is satisfactory to the player, he signs. If not he can go (or return) to college. This system seems to work well for players and owners. A player interested in turning pro does not have to risk his college eligibility, and guesswork about position in the draft is eliminated. If a player is picked by a team after high school, he can weigh the contract offer against the perceived benefit of attending a four-year college for at least three years or a junior college for at least one year.

According to MLB rules, a team that drafts a player "retains the rights to sign a selected player until 11:59 PM (EDT) August 15, or until the player enters, or returns to, a four-year college on a full-time basis. A player who is drafted and does not sign with the Club that selected him may be drafted again at a future year's Draft, so long as the player is eligible for that year's Draft. A Club may not select a player again in a subsequent year, unless the player has consented to the re-selection." Also, "A selected player who enters a junior college cannot be signed until the conclusion of the school's baseball season."

NFL Draft

Number of rounds: 7 (approximately 255 draftees; teams who lose free agents are awarded additional picks as compensation)
When: Late April

A player is first eligible for the NFL draft three years past his high school graduation. The rule barring "underage" players from the NFL has been tested in the courts, but to date no player has prevailed. The courts have found that a league, with the express agreement of its players association, can set minimum age requirements.

NCAA rules allow Division I-A and I-AA football players to declare for the NFL Draft one time during their collegiate careers without jeopardizing eligibility in that sport. But there's a huge caveat. Unlike an NBA prospect, an NFL prospect can return to his college team only if he is not selected by an NFL team. In the NBA, a player can "test the waters," get a better idea of his likely draft position, then make an informed decision to either remain in the draft or withdraw. An NFL prospect does not have that luxury. Once he declares for the NFL Draft, he can return only if he is not selected in the seven rounds of the draft (and provided he has followed all NCAA rules).

An NFL evaluation

If you are an underclassman eligible for the NFL draft, you can request an evaluation from an NFL advisory committee to gauge where you are likely to be drafted. The committee is made up of 12 NFL scouts and executives, along with representatives from two scouting services employed by NFL teams.

The committee provides one of five assessments. The player either:

- will be drafted in round one.
- will not be drafted higher than the second round.
- will not be drafted higher than the fourth round.
- will not be drafted higher than the sixth round.
- will not be drafted.

The committee points out that this is a "good faith opinion" and "in no way a commitment or guarantee of any player's selection."

NHL Draft

Number of rounds: 7 (210 draftees)
When: June

There is a lottery held for the first 14 picks in the NHL Draft.

Eligibility: Players must turn 18 by September 15, but cannot be older than 20 by December 31. Non-North American players must be 20. Players who are 18 do not "opt in" to the draft. They are automatically eligible for selection. Since 2004, 18-year-old players from NCAA Division I schools can be drafted and retain their college eligibility as long as they don't play for a pro team or hire an agent.

A player not signed by his NHL team within two years of being drafted can reenter the draft, as long as he is 20 years old or younger at the time of the subsequent draft. NCAA players are an exception: NHL teams retain the rights to a college player until 30 days after the player has left college. However, the latest NHL collective bargaining agreement offers an incentive to players who stay in college for four years: If a drafted player stays in college until his class graduates, he becomes an unrestricted free agent on August 15 of that year.

NBA Draft

Number of rounds: 2 (60 draftees)
When: Late June

Beginning in 2006, the minimum age for entering the draft increased from 18 to 19 (as of draft day). Underclassmen must declare for the draft by the end of April by notifying the commissioner's office in writing. NCAA rules grant college basketball players a one-time opportunity to declare for the draft but return to their college teams, under the following circumstances (you must satisfy both conditions):

1. You withdraw your name from consideration at least 10 days prior to the draft or you are not drafted, and
2. You follow all NCAA rules regarding amateurism, agents and academics (summarized in the five "don'ts" and one "do" in Chapter 2)

An NBA evaluation

Similar to the NFL, underclass basketball players contemplating going pro can request an evaluation from an NBA advisory committee. The committee provides a consensus opinion as to where they believe a player is likely to be drafted (e.g., lottery pick, first round, second round, not expected to be drafted).

The recommendation includes the following caveat: "The Committee's evaluation is only an educated assessment and is not binding in any way or a commitment or guarantee that a player will or will not be drafted in a certain slot or at all."

Testing NBA waters

If you decide to apply for the NBA Draft, but you're not 100% sure of your decision, you should do everything you can to keep your options open. Simple advice, but not necessarily easy to follow when you add in NCAA (and perhaps your college's) rules on extra benefits, agents and academics. Most agents and others who may try to influence you are not well versed in NCAA rules, so do not accept their advice as gospel.

Here are four things to consider if you want to use the rule allowing an athlete to return to school to your advantage:

1. *Follow NCAA rules regarding eligibility, agents and amateurism.* Trying out for the NBA means significant time away from school, which could impact your academic eligibility. When it comes to NCAA rules, proceed with caution. NCAA rules make you accountable for your actions as well as actions by your family and actions by agents. Advise your family members and advisers to do nothing, take nothing and make no commitments without consulting you first.

2. *Document everything.* To protect you and your school from NCAA backlash, make your intentions known in writing so that there is no misunderstanding. And keep a copy on file! If an NBA team invites you to work

out, NCAA rules now allow teams to pay your actual and necessary expenses, including airfare, hotel and meals, provided the trip lasts no longer than 48 hours and you do not miss class. If you pay your own way, the time restriction does not apply, but you must not miss class. (The NBA Pre-Draft Camp is exempted from the 48-hour time limitation).

3. *Communicate with your college coach.* Don't burn bridges. The rule allowing an athlete to test his pro potential with the option to return to school is great for you, but potentially disruptive to your coach and to athletes he is recruiting. Think about it from your coach's perspective: while you "test the waters," the coach doesn't know whether you will return or not, putting his recruiting program in limbo.

4. *Appoint a point person.* Since NCAA rules prohibit student athletes from hiring an agent to market their athletic services, you need to have someone coordinate your pre-draft activities. The NCAA limits your options to a parent or legal guardian, your coach or someone from your school's professional sports counseling panel. A parent or college coach can arrange tryouts with NBA teams for any bona-fide prospect. If he is supportive of your decision to test the waters, your college coach can be invaluable in contacting NBA general managers and scouts.

Final words: If you have any questions, contact the NBA and/or the NBPA, your school's compliance officer, and/or the NCAA for advice specific to your situation.

"I'm back." Well, not exactly.

After Randolph Morris' sophomore season at Kentucky, he declared himself for the 2005 NBA Draft, but was not selected. He thought he could return to play for his school, as permitted by NCAA rules. But Morris was ruled ineligible for the entire season (later reduced to 14 games) because, in the eyes of the NCAA, he had an agent working on his behalf, and because he did not pay all his own expenses associated with working out for NBA teams.

Another lesson from this case: A player is eligible for the NBA draft only once. After that, he can enter the league as an undrafted free agent. Less than a week after he played his final collegiate game of the 2006-07 season, Morris signed a two-year, $1.6-million contract with the New York Knicks.

How to Work the Draft

I remember when ESPN first came to the league and proposed putting the [NFL] draft on television. [NFL commissioner] Pete Rozelle, as much as a visionary as he was, said, "Why?"
—Ernie Accorsi, retired NFL executive

Chapter highlights

- Do your best to prepare for the draft, but don't let it drive you crazy.
- Being a good character guy helps.
- Opportunities to play pro sports exist outside the U.S.

The science of the draft is far from foolproof, but it is helpful to have an understanding of how the process works. Draft position is important, especially in terms of guaranteed money, but do not sweat details that fall beyond your control. Do your best to prepare for the draft, then show up day one ready to work hard whether you've been drafted by your dream team or by your least-favorite organization. Remember: It's not where you start, but where you *finish* your career.

Twenty years ago nobody put such emphasis on The Draft. Then ESPN and TNT began providing wall-to-wall coverage of the NFL and NBA drafts. In 2007, NFL Network aired 16 episodes of *Path to the Draft*, a three-part draft preview, plus several draft-themed shows on *NFL Total Access*. ESPN and the NFL Network aired first-to-last-pick coverage live from Radio City Music Hall in New York. The NFL and NBA drafts have been televised since the mid-1980s. In 2007 ESPN started televising the MLB Draft, which takes place in midseason and sends players to the minor leagues. Not all 50 rounds. Yet.

The draft represents hope for bad teams and their suffering fans. Unlike free agency, which favors rich teams, the draft is democratic, with teams drafting in reverse order to where they finished. A team which finished in the cellar can turn its fortunes around with one great pick or with a succession of good ones.

Fans have developed an insatiable appetite for all things related to the draft. The draft even has its own lingo, including quick-twitch muscles, relative value, shoulder-pad speed, tweener, stiff hips, locker-room presence, character issues, a reach, a project. "Draftniks" dissect every player and scenario. Countless publications, from *ESPN The Magazine and Sporting News* to the more arcane *Pro Football Weekly* break down the draft with the minute detail that *CNBC, The Wall Street Journal* and *Barron's* devote to coverage of the financial markets. In fact, the draft has come to resemble the stock market, where rumors, hype and speculation often trump fundamentals and change fortunes.

Professional sports leagues require prospects to try out prior to the draft. In the NFL, the most significant tryouts are the NFL Combine (in Indianapolis) and Pro Days which take place on college campuses. In the NBA, it's the Orlando Pre-Draft Camp. Probable first-round picks are also invited to work out privately for teams. Before the mid 1990s, draft prospects generally trained at their schools. Now, many attend combine camps such as the Athletes Performance Institute, which has facilities in Arizona and California.

Train like there's no tomorrow

With so much money at stake, many draft-eligible athletes quite reasonably spend 100% of their time and energy preparing for the draft. They begin to train soon after their last college game ends. This has led to more players dropping out of school during the second semester.

To their credit, many athletes are putting themselves on 3- or 3.5-year graduation tracks, knowing that they plan to get a degree and leave school early to get a head start on draft preparation. **Now that the NCAA permits athletes to attend summer school before their freshman year, athletes can easily get on a faster graduation track.**

Draft prospects, even those projected for selection in the lower rounds, expect their agents to pay for their training. Depending on its nature and duration, training can cost as much as $20,000. Representing athletes who are not sure-fire early picks can be an expensive proposition for an agent.

Many pro teams administer psychological and intelligence tests. In addition to working on athletic skills and physical conditioning, players now prep for the intelligence tests and for being interviewed, including going through intense mock interviews. There is even a book on mastering the 40-yard dash that lists 832 ways to lower your 40-yard dash time.

Gaming the draft

Put yourself in the shoes of the people who decide whether to draft you and, if so, how high. General managers' jobs depend on putting the right players on their rosters. Owners compete with other owners to make the right multimillion-dollar investments. Tiny differences between players get magnified. Therefore, do everything you can to be what the GMs, coaches and owners are looking for. You may place high in mock drafts, or an agent may tell you he's got the pull to make you a No. 1 pick. Don't believe the hype. Things can and do change in a heartbeat, and only the real draft counts. One bad workout can move you from 3 to 17, or from sixth round (NFL) to not drafted.

You want to arrive in Orlando (NBA Pre-draft Camp) or Indianapolis (NFL Combine) full of confidence based on preparation. Use the off-season to sharpen your skills, strength, and conditioning. Be willing to invest in a skill and/or strength and conditioning coach or in a pre-draft camp. (Your agent may initially pay for this, but ultimately you pay for these services through fees.) Work on your people skills, too. Studies have shown that management hires people it likes and respects. Act in a way that gets you labeled as a hard worker, a team player and a learner. Being viewed as self-indulgent, high-maintenance and untrainable is bad business.

To maintain a little humility, while it is a tremendous feat to play sports at the professional level, keep in mind that athletes are replaceable commodities. Even without Michael Jordan playing, the NBA still operates at a profit. There are about 3,900 professional athletes in the NFL, NBA, NHL and MLB combined; there are 100 times as many people who would kill (figuratively, I hope) or cheat (literally) for that same opportunity.

Habits count

Coaches and GMs are paid to win championships. They draft "character guys" mainly because off-the-field incidents are huge disruptions. From the commissioner's office point of view, character guys help the marketing of the entire league.

Team owners and managers believe—based on a great deal of evidence—that habits, good and bad, are unlikely to change. A player with a weight problem will probably continue to struggle with weight. Yes, Charles Barkley, the "Round Mound of Rebound" in college, got his weight under control and went on to enjoy a Hall of Fame pro career. But John "Hot Plate" Williams, Stanley Roberts and Oliver Miller couldn't lose the extra pounds and didn't last very long in the NBA. GMs play the percentages. Among players of apparently equal ability, they will downgrade those with a history of legal, physical or attitude problems.

Some elite college athletes make mistakes involving off-the-field/court behavior. Let's hope they learn from their mistakes and move on. Unfortunately, it's not as simple as issuing a *mea culpa*. When it comes to your career as a professional athlete, you will be held accountable for your past mistakes, often including the ones you thought you got away with.

Big Brother is watching

"The NFL has its own private investigation firm. It is called NFL Security...[if] you're a college football player looking to join the NFL, the security office knows you exist. A primary function of the 40-man force is to dig up facts about possible draftees. If a player smokes marijuana at Saturday-night parties, it's probably in his file. If he brawls with neighbors, it's probably in his file. Investigators are particularly interested in the old standbys: illegal drugs, unsavory associations and sports gambling."
—Sports Illustrated, April 15, 1996

We'll never fully understand why some guys make it and others do not. The chance to play professional sports is so slim that increasing the odds in your favor by good, clean living is a smart—and safe—bet.

Pro opportunities beyond the U.S. leagues

Growing up in America, athletes dream of playing in the big leagues. Go for it. But it's not the be-all, end-all. The very long odds against becoming a pro athlete become a bit more favorable when you look beyond the NBA, NFL, MLB, NHL, WNBA, Professional Golfers Assn. (PGA), LPGA, Assn. of Tennis Professionals (ATP), or Women's Tennis Assn. (WTA). I left Major League Soccer (MLS) off this list because from the international point of view, professional soccer in the U.S. is "second division," with salaries—other than David Beckham's—to match.

Financial rewards outside the big leagues may not be as astronomical, but they can be high enough for an athlete to accumulate several million dollars, particularly in the upper-level professional basketball leagues in Spain, Italy and Greece, and in Japanese baseball. While many players are reluctant to go abroad, many others have gone on to lucrative, fulfilling careers playing overseas. Some have made the move when they were not drafted; others after or even in the middle of U.S. pro careers. The following account by point guard Tyus Edney, who helped UCLA win the NCAA championship in 1995, highlights the benefits and challenges of playing overseas.

From the NBA to Europe to the NBA to Europe

After college I played two seasons with the Sacramento Kings and one with the Boston Celtics. The NBA is a great deal for those who can sign long-term contracts, but many players don't enjoy that security. I played for a Lithuanian team, Zalgiris Kaunas, for the 1998-99 season, the year of the NBA lockout. I wasn't under contract with an NBA team, so it wasn't worth waiting to see if I would hook up with one.

Going overseas to play basketball was not necessarily my first choice. I didn't know what to expect. It was huge that my UCLA teammate and good friend George Zidek was on the team. The first couple of months took some getting used to, but it got easier.

In 1999-2000, I played in Italy, for Benneton Treviso. I returned to the NBA in 2000-01 and played for the Indiana Pacers. Then I went back to Benetton Treviso, where Mike D'Antoni (now coach of the Phoenix Suns) was the coach. [Benetton Treviso won back- to-back championships, and Edney was named 2002 All-Europe Import Player of the Year by Eurobasket.com.]

It's definitely a cultural adjustment when you visit another country, and more so when you move there as a professional athlete. Even though English is widely spoken in most other countries, it's important to pick up the country's native language. It helps you fit in; without it you feel disconnected.

Some may think playing in Europe is a step down in skill level, but it's not. It's probably where the NBA was 20-30 years ago in terms of marketing, but not when it comes to abilities. It's just different. European leagues play 50, maybe 60 games. We practice a lot, even twice a day during the season. Because there aren't as many games, the regular season games are important. It's like a college atmosphere, which is great.

Even those of us who don't sign big NBA contracts can make a lot of money playing ball. It makes sense for some to hold out until an NBA offer comes or even to play in the D-League, but don't limit yourself. Be proactive. If you get a decent offer to play in Europe, it's more an opportunity than a step down.

There are risks going overseas. You hear stories about Euro teams that don't meet their payrolls or don't pay on time or at all. Find out their reputation and who is backing the team. Try not to leave yourself exposed (at a minimum, get an open-ended return flight home) and stay on top of things.

—Tyus Edney

Part Three

THE BUSINESS OF YOUR LIFE

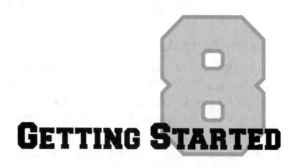

GETTING STARTED

There was a time when a fool and his money were soon parted,
but now it happens to everybody.
—Adlai E. Stevenson, Illinois governor,
U.S. Presidential Candidate in 1952 and 1956

Chapter highlights

- Learn the jargon of business and investing.
- Don't try to keep up with the Joneses when it comes to spending.
- Maximize earnings, minimize spending, invest conservatively, select great advisers.

Introduction

As a professional athlete, you are among the fortunate few who can earn a lot of money at a young age. Unfortunately, that does not automatically translate into a happy and satisfying life. Many athletes, entertainers, lottery winners and others who hit the jackpot have discovered that sudden wealth can even bring on misery—such as when you have to deal with family members, friends and "long-lost friends" who want a share. This section helps you take advantage of the opportunities—and avoid the disasters—associated with high income, fame and (let's hope) growing fortune.

You will make some financial mistakes. Everyone does, including professional athletes. Let's hope you will use the information that follows to help minimize your mistakes and maximize your financial success.

Business talk

This section includes some investment jargon. You will not be tested. However, familiarity with these terms will help prepare you to handle your financial affairs. If you want more information, you're just a click away on Google or Wikipedia, among other sources. Better to read about this stuff at your own pace and have time to digest it, than to hear it first from a stockbroker or financial adviser talking a mile a minute. Many, but not all, of the following terms are used in this section. Some are defined, at least through context:

> Active vs. passive management, amortization, annuity, asset allocation, assets, bear/bull markets, benchmarks, bonds, churning, commodities, compounding, dividend yield, due diligence, equity, fiduciary, gold, hedging, index, indexing, inflation, internal rate of return (IRR), investment grade, IRA, leverage, liabilities, long/short fund, margin, mortgage, NASDAQ, NYSE, PE ratio, pension, Ponzi scheme, principal, private equity, risk/return tradeoff, ROE, ROI, Roth IRA, Sarbanes-Oxley, SEC, S&P 500 Index, stocks, T-Bills, tax deferred, vesting, volatility, withholding tax, yield, yield to maturity. (OK, I am out of breath.)

Financial success/failure

I have identified four main factors that determine financial success—or, on the flipside, financial failure. They are (1) income, (2) spending, (3) investing and (4) selection of financial and legal advisers.

You don't have to be an expert—it is hoped that the people you hire will be the experts. But a basic understanding of these areas will give you the ability to ask the experts the right questions, supervise them, help them perform best for you, and help you make the best decisions.

Income

If you don't make money, you will have a tough time amassing wealth. Fortunately, you not only chose a very lucrative profession, but you beat the long odds to gain entry into one of the smallest work forces around—professional sports.

Compensation, whether you're a blue-collar laborer or a professional athlete, is largely a function of market forces. You don't control the market, but you can influence your position within it by performing at the highest level possible. That gives you two reasons to work hard at your sport: because you enjoy what you're doing and you like to win, and because you want to maximize earnings (another way to win). When it comes to endorsement income, you either have marketing appeal or you don't. If you have appeal, you can either enhance it or diminish it. Most endorsement dollars flow to sports figures who are likable, trustworthy, engaging and law-abiding. While you are the one most responsible for creating your own market value, you likely will need to hire legal and financial professionals to help you maximize your full earning potential.

Spending

While the market plays a major role in determining your compensation, you are pretty much in control of what you spend. The more you save, the better. To paraphrase an old Chicago political credo: Save early and save often. Many people assume they will make more later, so they spend more than they make. This is a formula for disaster. As novelist Charles Dickens wrote in *A Tale of Two Cities*, "Annual income twenty pounds, annual expenditure nineteen six, result happiness. Annual income twenty pounds, annual expenditure twenty pounds ought and six, result misery."

Investing

The more money you invest, the more money you should earn from your investments. This may sound like a "Yogi-ism" (New York Yankees Hall of Fame catcher Yogi Berra is perhaps best known for his unmistakable quotes), but here goes: You don't make money by making money. You make money by saving (and investing) the money you make.

Selecting advisers

As the next two chapters will show, your ability to select honest, accountable, competent, and qualified financial and legal professionals will significantly impact your bottom line. Your net worth will be largely determined by the company you keep.

> *When someone asks to borrow money: "I'll see what my lawyer says...And if he says yes, I'll find another lawyer."*
> —W.C. Fields

Get smart about your spending

In the next several chapters, you will read a lot about how to improve the chances that you will select the right business advisers, how to invest, and how to prepare for success beyond professional sports. All worthwhile information. It's meaningless, however, if you fail to establish—and follow—a sensible budget.

The window for earning large sums of money for professional athletes is typically narrow. Yes, you might make great money today. And it's also probable that you will sign at least one more lucrative contract. But probable doesn't mean absolute. The reality about money: Until your net worth is at least 20 times your annual spending (which puts you in a position to live off interest and/or returns without tapping principal), you aren't financially secure.

Based on your annual living expenses, here's what you need to bank:

Annual expenses	Net worth
$100,000	$2 million
$200,000	$4 million
$500,000	$10 million
$1,000,000	$20 million

Having a million-dollar lifestyle is worthwhile only if it is supported by your own net worth, not by lenders, who will extract a "pound of flesh" if you miss a debt payment.

Fun and fortune

Some of the advice I offer might not sound like fun. You can live on a self-imposed budget, hold off on some big-ticket purchases, invest prudently—and still enjoy life. It may mean not buying something you really want (and can afford) today, despite having cash and credit available. But you can live like a king relative to the average American. The problem comes when you're an averaged-salaried professional athlete and you try to live beyond your means.

The short, simple guide to financial success:

➤ Pay off all credit card debt.
➤ Fund your 401(k) and other available retirement accounts to the max.

- Use my "Rule of 10" when it comes to budgeting: Each year in professional sports is roughly equivalent to 10 years working in the real world, so base spending on your current salary divided by 10.
- Include all financial help to friends and family, and contributions to charity, in your Rule of 10 budget.
- Hire good, competent, ethical business advisers.
- Do not give anyone full power of attorney.
- Buy the insurance you need (car, term-life, liability, etc.), not the most highly commissioned products.
- Make a will.
- Do not invest money you cannot afford to lose in nightclubs, restaurants, record labels and other risky propositions.
- Learn about business. Read *The Wall Street Journal.* Take advantage of educational opportunities offered by your league and players association. Hang out with business leaders, not salesmen.
- If a proposition sounds too good to be true, it probably is.
- Live modestly. Invest conservatively (8–12% annual returns are great). Have patience.
- As the old Prell shampoo label read, "Rinse. Repeat." Keep doing these things for years and even decades.

Pretty simple, right? That's the point.

Of course, there are details. Read on.

IF I'M THE ONLY PLAYER ON THIS TEAM WHO'S
GETTING HIT, THEN YOU BETTER MAKE ME RICH!

BUILD YOUR TEAM

You can't watch everybody, and when you can't watch everybody, watch out.
—MC Hammer, hip-hop star, former Oakland A's batboy

Chapter highlights

$

- Understand the functions of business, financial and legal professionals.
- Learn how to oversee your team.
- Be a good client.

Some people may tell you, "Focus on your sport. We'll take care of the rest." True, you can and should hire people to do things on your behalf, from providing you with legal and financial advice to preparing complicated documents to running errands. But, when you hire people, you should understand what they're doing, how much they're charging, and how you will benefit more than if you did it yourself. Don't tempt people to take advantage of you by not paying attention to how they are handling, or spending, your money.

Hiring an agent is typically your first "draft pick" as you build your team. Then you need to add other qualified, competent legal and financial professionals. The process suggested for hiring a sports agent described in Chapter 5 can work well for hiring any professional adviser.

A team cannot succeed without the right combination of good players. The team of You, Inc., is no exception. You are the general manager in charge of hiring (and if necessary, firing) the players. You build your team to win. Winning means you

➤ Make more money.
➤ Keep more money.
➤ Reduce risk.
➤ Save time and energy.

Hire the right players and you can accomplish these goals. Hire the wrong players and you may never get there. With bad advisers you could pay a lot of money and get nothing in return or, worse, you could end up in a tangled business arrangement that costs money, time and energy to escape from.

First I'll describe the types of professionals often employed by pro athletes, then I'll talk about how to hire those who will perform best for you.

> **Money Players Warning:**
> Selection of lawyers or financial advisers whose greatest qualification is their friendship with you can lead to financial ruin, tax and legal troubles, depression, anxiety and anger.

Lawyers

Even if you have a great agent who negotiates your playing contract, you may need the services of legal specialists in the following situations:

- Estate planning. No one wants to think about dying, but everybody does. Once you start making a lot of money, it's your responsibility to prepare for every eventuality, even the one that doesn't include you.
- Business transactions. When you enter into a partnership, buy or sell a business or home, or invest in real estate, you will probably need the services of a lawyer who specializes in these areas.
- Children, marriage, divorce. Consult with a family lawyer at pivotal points in your life as a parent or spouse. We all hope love will prevail, but if it doesn't, at least the fair share of your money will be protected.

Financial adviser

The money you save should be protected and earning income for you. A financial adviser should help you invest your money wisely. A good adviser will help you take reasonable risk for reasonable return. As one former professional athlete observed, "An agent can screw an athlete by signing a bad playing contract, say, $2.7 million instead of $3 million. A bad financial adviser can blow every penny." Financial advisers come under a variety of headings, including financial planner, money manager, investment manager and stockbroker.

Accountant

The catchphrase from the hit 1996 movie Jerry Maguire was, "Show me the money." Having a good certified public accountant (CPA), one you can trust, is paramount in business, particularly when money is flowing in many directions and multiple people may have access to your accounts.

Your accountant should advise you how, within the limits of the law, to structure your financial dealings to minimize taxes. Of course, the accountant will also prepare your tax returns. A good accountant will also ensure that your financial records are organized, your taxes are filed on time, and you are in good shape to survive an audit.

Some sports agencies and money management firms have in-house CPAs to handle client taxes, a practice I do not support. Your CPA should have allegiance only to you, and act as a check and balance on the other professionals on your team.

Business manager

Most business managers are CPAs or lawyers or are associated with an accounting firm. Musicians, actors, directors, writers and producers have worked with business managers for decades. Business managers typically provide the same services as accountants, but provide many additional services, including:

- Evaluate potential business deals.
- Negotiate purchases of "big ticket" items such as houses and cars, and obtain financing.
- Collect and audit licensing royalties and endorsement payments.
- Oversee other financial and legal professionals.
- Uncover discrepancies, if any.
- Pay bills.
- Store legal and financial records.

A business manager typically charges a percentage of the client's income with a cap (maximum) set in dollars, based on the services to be provided. You have to be a high earner to justify the expense, but competent business managers should ultimately more than pay for themselves. Particularly at the start of your career, the counseling provided by a good business manager can prove invaluable, along with the business manager's network of professionals who are known to be trustworthy, expert team players.

The use of business managers among professional athletes is not widespread, perhaps because many view these services as fungible (the less you pay, the better) rather than value-added (can save you more money and time than it costs).

Business managers operate outside the legal jurisdiction of players associations. Thus an unscrupulous business manager can find it relatively easy to take advantage of a client. Evaluate the relative merits of paying someone on an hourly basis to perform services compared to hiring a business manager. Also, consider having a lawyer review any personal services or business management contracts.

Insurance broker/agent

Your financial plan is likely to call for buying disability insurance, so that getting injured or seriously ill is less of a catastrophic financial loss. Your estate plan is likely to include buying life insurance. A good life insurance broker will help you get the most value for your dollars in purchasing life and disability policies, and will help keep you properly insured as your financial and family situations change.

To insure your property (house, car, boat, et al.) and protect yourself against liability (someone suing you), you'll need another insurance professional who specializes in property and liability insurance.

Personal services

There are only 24 hours in a day, and many of them are already assigned to practice, fitness training, games and travel. How much is your time worth? You may want to hire a housekeeper and/or a part-time personal assistant. Personal assistants can do a wide variety of tasks, including errands, shopping, fielding phone calls, keeping your social calendar, and planning parties and other events. "Superstar" athletes typically have such a busy schedule that employing a full-time assistant is a necessity, even if it costs $50,000 or more a year. Unfortunately, many average-salaried athletes are beginning to do the same without considering the costs of this luxury. **A full-time personal assistant can hinder athletes from becoming self-sufficient.**

In 2007, "celebrity" Paris Hilton was sentenced to 45 days in jail for violating the terms of her parole for a previous drunk driving offense, which included a ban on driving. Hilton admitted to the judge that she did not read the terms of her probation, but instead relied on her personal assistant, who apparently left out that important detail. Oops.

How to work with your professional adviser team

Do the research on the front end, so that you have the highest probability of hiring the right advisers to begin with. Then develop good relationships with them, and encourage them to work well with each other.

You may want to appoint a "point person" or "quarterback" responsible for making sure everyone on your team is working together to accomplish your goals, that information is shared, and that nothing is falling through the cracks. We have all seen a ball fall between two baseball players, each of whom thought the other was going to catch it. You do not want your business affairs to resemble that sorry scenario. Agents, with whom athletes typically have the most interaction, often serve as point persons.

Coordination of business functions

Various advisory functions can overlap. Each team member should understand his or her role, and should work to support the group's efforts to achieve your goals. Sometimes business people get territorial about their work and do not appreciate others questioning it. But competent professionals who act in their clients' best interests should not have a problem when questioned by fellow team members.

If your team is working well, you should be confident that tax strategy is integrated into your contracts and investments, and you should periodically receive:

➤ spending budgets
➤ financial statements that measure key variables (such as your liquid net worth and the gain or loss of each of your investments) in a way that you can easily understand and follow, including all fees and commissions
➤ state and federal income tax returns (annual and, if required, estimated taxes four times a year)

If you're actively involved with your business and financial affairs and you have controls in place to ensure everything is handled properly, you should be able to determine whether you're receiving quality service. If that's not the case, take action.

You can't always quantify how much a financial or legal professional makes or saves you. Let's say your lawyer writes a well-conceived and well-crafted legal agreement. You see the bill, but you may never be aware of the loss of money and the aggravation you might have suffered if the agreement had been done poorly. When it comes to investments, if there is good reporting, the numbers don't lie. Even in this arena, however, you don't necessarily know how alternative investments would have worked out and it may take years to evaluate the results of a particular investment or investment strategy. Remember, if in doubt, ask until you are satisfied with the answer.

Be a good client

I talked a lot about what to look for in the advisers you hire, but to maximize the value of your business relationships, you also have to be—to borrow a sports cliché—"on the ball." Help your advisers do a good job for you. When they call or email, respond. If they need documents signed and returned, get it done. Keep in mind that if you're lax about your business affairs, you give everyone around you license to do the same. And this all comes at your expense. Literally.

Feel free to criticize an adviser if you believe he or she has failed to do something or has done something wrong. If you're not sure, start by asking a question. Even if you are sure, be diplomatic. Conversely, praise an adviser who does consistent good work or has done something outstanding. Yes, that's what you're paying them for, but advisers—like anyone else—want to know their good work is appreciated, and tend to "go the extra mile" for clients who express appreciation. For similar reasons, when you receive a correct invoice from an adviser, pay it promptly.

DO THE DUE DILIGENCE

Believe nothing, no matter where you read it, or who said it—even if I said it
—unless it agrees with your own reason and your own common sense.

—Buddha

Chapter highlights

- Trust, but verify.
- Don't believe the sales hype.
- Read the fine print. And believe it.

Perhaps the biggest mistake you can make as a professional athlete is to act based on trusting unethical, deceitful, ignorant or incompetent people. Athletes who have made such mistakes have seen their careers end, relationships with loved ones destroyed, and millions of dollars go up in smoke.

The best way to avoid such consequences is to question people's claims rather than accept them at face value. Do your homework or, as they say in the business world, "exercise due diligence." Your parents and/or trusted advisers can help in this regard, especially when it comes to asking the tough questions.

This approach applies to all kinds of situations: being pitched by a financial adviser about the high rate of return he will deliver; listening to a fellow athlete tell you how much money you will make if you become a partner in his restaurant start-up; being urged by a trainer to take some pills to improve your performance; getting a plea from a charity—even being told how wonderful you are by a beautiful woman you met at a bar.

Every one of the above could be truthful, well-informed and well-intentioned. Unless you exercise due diligence, however, you won't know. You should know that many—perhaps most—such claims are false. All the hard work you did to become a pro athlete has made you a target for fraudsters and incompetents. You owe it to yourself to make sure they miss their target.

"We're just artful liars"

Professional athletes are not financial mavens, even if they have gone to college. Most begin with the concept that most people are good, honest and hard-working. In fact, that is usually true. But there a few bad ones who cause disproportionate harm.

People who commit fraud are the ones who appear to be the most trustworthy. Later you find out we're just artful liars. We're friendly and outgoing. We take your humanity for others and exploit it. Our job is deceitful, but trustworthiness is an absolute necessity for someone who wants to successfully con people out of money.

We don't want to be around people who are skeptical or diligent. If you're pressing for specific answers, we usually go away. Why deal with someone who is going to question our ethics? There are too many other easy marks out there who won't.

—Sam Antar, former Crazy Eddie chief financial officer, convicted felon

> *The large print giveth and the*
> *small print taketh away.*
> —Tom Waits, American singer/songwriter

Read the fine print

Despite government regulations requiring full disclosure, a lot of investment sales literature still paints rosy pictures of wonderful returns with seemingly minimal risk. Or at least that's what the colorful charts and graphs and endorsements are designed to convey. The smaller print contains the (often scary) disclaimers, which always include (because the Securities and Exchange Commission requires it), these words: "Past performance is no guarantee of future results." Sam Antar recommends not just reading an investment prospectus, but *studying* it.

Verbal pitches for investments are often more exaggerated and one-sided than written sales materials, because they are easy to deny in a court case or arbitration hearing. If you hear someone describe a return as "guaranteed," and it's not a Federal Deposit Insurance Corporation (FDIC)-insured bank account, run like hell. Higher-than-average returns are a reward for taking risks.

Where the money is

When the infamous thief Willie Sutton was asked why he robbed banks, he said, "Because that's where the money is." For the exact same reason, crooks target professional athletes. Young, financially inexperienced and often surrounded by "yes" people, professional athletes are magnets for scam artists. Instead of holding a gun on you, they get you to willingly, even eagerly, hand over your money.

Kirk Wright, founder of hedge fund International Management Associates (IMA), is among the latest scammers to be accused of defrauding current and former pro athletes. From 1998 to 2005, which as *The Wall Street Journal* pointed out included the worst bear market (a market in which most stocks or other investments declined) since the Great Depression, Wright reported phenomenal average annual returns of more than 27%. The returns apparently were fabricated. The SEC estimates that Wright bilked investors out of at least $115 million.

Wright partnered with former anesthesiologists Nelson Bond and Fitz Harper Jr., who helped win over medical doctors. He also hired former Denver Broncos football star Steve Atwater as an investment adviser. An SEC complaint filed in February 2006 claims that Atwater invested $2.8 million of his own money in IMA. Atwater helped raise approximately $15 million from his NFL friends, including Blaine Bishop, Terrell Davis and Rod Smith. Atwater lost a lot of his own money, and appears to be a victim as well as perhaps an unwitting accomplice.

In February 2007, a Georgia federal judge entered a default judgment against Wright, who was ordered to pay nearly $20 million. As of March 2007, Wright was being held in federal custody awaiting trial for criminal fraud charges.

Unfortunately, professional athletes are frequent victims of unscrupulous agents and financial advisers.

According to the NFL Players Assn., from 1999 through 2002, 78 NFL players lost a total of at least $42 million as a result of criminal fraud. This figure only covers then-active NFL players, only those who reported the fraud, and does not include the Wright case. And it does not account for losses resulting from unsuitable investments (often with high commissions or referral fees) recommended by incompetent and/or unethical financial advisers that did not result in fraud convictions.

What can pro athletes (and others) do to increase the chances that they are not wronged by the next Mr. Wright?

Demand answers you can understand, and walk away if you don't get them. Marketing materials for Wright's IMA stated that the fund's "objectives are achieved through a top-down, bottom-up process that identifies disparities in the economy or security sectors creating +/- changes in market perception." Medical doctors as well as athletes nodded their heads at this gobbledygook and pulled out their checkbooks.

Don't believe the hype. Wright's alleged illegal activities were abetted by investors' get-rich-quick dreams. The competitive makeup of professional athletes, doctors and even savvy businessmen often lead them to take huge risks in hopes of achieving spectacular returns. Pro athletes are not wired to "play it safe." Historically, consistent 8-12% investment returns are superb, but psychologically it's hard to resist the impulse to chase bigger, faster, stronger returns.

Investigate track records. The dazzling returns that Mr. Wright and IMA claimed went unchallenged by those who invested in his hedge fund. Professional athletes and others should not entrust their money to anyone without verifying that the financial information provided is accurate. Numbers do lie, but they lie less when compiled by a reputable CPA firm known in the investment community. Invest only in deals where the financial statements have been audited by a top-tier firm. No exceptions.

Don't jump into hedge funds. Because (as of 2007) hedge funds are less regulated than many other forms of investment, the SEC mandates that the net worth of hedge investors must exceed "$1,000,000 or [have] individual income in excess of $200,000 in each of the two most recent years." The theory is that millionaires are financially more savvy and, therefore, do not need the government to protect them against unscrupulous or incompetent hedge fund managers.

As Wright's scam reveals, many non-financial professionals with net worths north of $1 million challenge the SEC's assumption. Professional athletes would be better off if they self-imposed a $5-million minimum on their investment capital before layering on riskier asset classes such as hedge funds.

Custody your money at a large, reputable, SEC-registered firm. If you hire an investment adviser to direct your investments, placing your money at a separate brokerage firm adds a critical layer of protection. According to the SEC complaint, Wright forged Ameritrade account statements. Simple steps to take:

➤ Deposit all money directly into an account with the custodian firm.
➤ Through the custodian, authorize the money manager to have the authority to trade but not withdraw money from your account.
➤ Have monthly account statements sent directly to you by the custodian.
➤ Establish direct online access to your account on the custodian's Web site, and check it regularly. (Especially important given how easy it is these days to create or modify authentic-looking documents.)

Good investments don't come neatly labeled

Objective financial information is more widely available today than ever before. Separating the good investments from the bad means taking an active interest in your financial affairs, including reading financial publications and seeking out business mentors. Ultimately, you do have to put a certain amount of trust in someone. But do so carefully and with controls to protect yourself from worst-case scenarios of fraud and incompetence.

As the admittedly financially unsavvy humorist Will Rogers once said, he was not "as concerned about return on investment as return of investment." Good advice.

Friends and family

Friends and family can help you achieve your goals—or they can drag you down. Should you hire friends and family members to be your professional service providers? Yes—if based on their experience, knowledge and ethics, they would be among the most qualified candidates even if they were not family or friends. Otherwise, you are likely to get burned financially...and your relationships will also go up in flames. Muhammad Ali, MC Hammer and many other well-known athletes and entertainers gave friends jobs and got burned for millions.

Friends and family members who you have reason to trust, and who are well-organized in their jobs and personal lives, often make great personal assistants. If you do hire a friend, make sure the money you pay is reasonable for the services provided.

Ask, ask, ask

The ability to read people may be the most important skill in personal relationships and in business. But none of us can accurately judge a person's ability or integrity simply by how they present themselves. You need to ask questions. It takes guts to challenge people to back up their statements, especially when they are financial or legal professionals who traditionally command respect. If you don't understand a reply, keep asking. You want an expert who can and will explain things to you so that you can make informed decisions.

In 1998, the National Futures Assn. (NFA) published a pamphlet, Investment Swindles: How They Work and How to Avoid Them. The publication lists several great questions aimed to repel swindlers. The following questions and comments are based on the NFA pamphlet:

What are the risks involved?
Except for obligations of the U.S. Treasury, all investments carry some risk of loss of principle.

Can you send me a written explanation of the proposed investment, including prospectus and/or risk disclosure statement, so I can study it at my leisure?
Most crooks will not put anything in writing that might cause them to run afoul of postal authorities or provide possible evidence in a fraud trial. Swindlers want your money now, not tomorrow or next week.

Would you mind explaining your investment proposal to some third party, such as my attorney, accountant, investment adviser or banker?
The salesperson may say something like, "Normally, I'd be glad to, but there isn't time for that," or may put pressure on you by wondering "why you can't you make your own investment decisions." Again, take this response as an important clue.

Can you provide references?
Not just a list of other investors who supposedly became fabulously wealthy (the names you get may be the salesman's boss or someone sitting at the next phone), but reputable and reliable recommendations such as a bank or well-known brokerage firm that you can easily contact.

Are the investments you are offering traded on a regulated exchange, such as a securities or futures exchange?
Some legitimate investments are regulated and some aren't, but fraudulent investments rarely are. Exchanges have strict rules designed to assure fair dealing and competitive price determination. If you are told this investment isn't subject to regulation, You will need to provide ongoing supervision.

How much of my money would go for commissions, management fees and the like?

And ask whether there will be additional charges, or whether the investment agreement involves any type of profit-sharing arrangement in which the firm's principals participate. Insist on specific answers, not glib and evasive responses such as "that's not important" or "what's really important is how much money you are going to make."

Power of attorney

"Power of attorney" grants another person (who does not have to be a lawyer) the legal right to act on someone's behalf in a specified manner—for example, negotiating a particular deal or making medical decisions if the sick or injured person is unable to do so. There are circumstances in which you will need to grant limited power of attorney. Unlimited power of attorney means the appointed person can do absolutely anything legal in your name. It is against the law to commit fraud or embezzle money, regardless of what legal powers the perpetrator has been granted. However, the chance of getting victimized by such a crime, or even by a bad decision, increases dramatically when limits are not put in place. There is never a reason to give anyone unlimited power of attorney.

To safeguard yourself when granting power of attorney to professionals working on your behalf, such as lawyers, agents and business managers, make sure you:

1. Carefully limit the powers granted.
2. Continue to make sure that their powers (and your legal rights) are not abused.

If someone is paying your bills, they should be allowed to make recurring payments to specified accounts that are only in your name. It is easy to set up cash-management systems to ensure that money is only paid from your accounts to specified accounts such as mortgages, car payments, utilities, cable TV, credit cards and brokerage accounts.

For non-recurring transactions, such as purchasing a new house or car or making investments, you should always require your written authorization.

Final word

Direct oversight and efficient checks and balances make it unlikely that you be will be victimized by fraud or mismanagement, and make it likely that if wrongdoing takes place, you will catch it early…before much damage is done.

A Trip Down ^BAD^ Memory Lane

It is the greed of the sucker that makes the hustler's skill pay.
—David Spanier, author and gambling expert

Chapter highlights

- Bad memories for others; good lessons for you.
- When offered huge profits at no risk, remember the name Charles Ponzi.
- Charles Barkley says a good guy is not necessarily a good adviser.

We all like to think that while others might be taken in by a scam, we possess "street smarts" and will see through it. In fact, intelligent, savvy people do make mistakes; no one is immune.

Due diligence done right

The vast majority of bad business decisions—and life decisions for that matter—result from insufficient analysis. The previous chapter stressed the importance of conducting proper due diligence on the front end, then continuing to monitor your business associates.

Watch your emotions

There are many factors in decision-making that can trip you up. One of the biggest is your emotions. A study shows that among individuals who manage their own money, sociopaths—people who are emotionally flat—get significantly better returns than investors who are psychologically normal. Why? Normal people get attached to their investments, find it hard to accept they made a bad investment, and hang on to their losers too long. They also find it hard to buy when the overall market or a particular industry or company is declining and everybody seems to be selling (which can be the best time to buy) or to sell when the overall market or a particular investment has been surging (which can be the best time to sell). A very successful investor, Benjamin Graham, wrote, "The investor's chief problem—and even his worst enemy—is likely to be himself." Do your best to avoid making emotional decisions about investments. Instead, try to think things through, be objective, and don't base decisions on what "everyone else" is doing.

The rest of this chapter is devoted to the history of scams, mostly in sports, but starting with perhaps the most infamous scheme of all time:

The original Ponzi scheme

Charles Ponzi is a name to remember next time someone enthusiastically tells you about the quick money he or she made from an investment. In 1920, Ponzi promised investors a 50% return in 45 days or "double your money" in 90 days. Some early investors did get the promised high returns, and suddenly people lined up to join the bonanza. Approximately 40,000 people invested a total of about $15 million (roughly $150 million in 2007 dollars).

Profits were supposed to be generated by buying international postal reply coupons in Europe and exchanging them at a higher price in the United States. In fact, early investors were paid off from the funds invested by later investors. Ultimately, Ponzi went bankrupt and, after years of litigation, investors got back on average about one third of their money. Ever since, such "pyramid schemes" have been called "Ponzi schemes."

Not every investment "opportunity" that relies on foolishness and greed is a Ponzi scheme or is even necessarily illegal. Perhaps the best recent example is the mania for buying Internet stocks in the 1990s. Millions of investors scooped up shares in any company that had "dot-com" in its name, regardless of whether it made profits or even had a reasonable hope of ever making profits. Other investors saw share prices increase dramatically, sometimes within days, and hopped on the bandwagon.

When others are making, seem to be making or say they are making huge returns (at least on paper), it's hard to settle for a steady 5-10% per year, even if you know that's all you need to be financially secure for life. The promise of fast money trumps logic, especially when friends and teammates energetically participate.

If there is any doubt about the importance of selecting the right financial and legal advisers and making good financial decisions, these stories should prove educational…and entertaining.

"Steep tuition" for "crash course in business school"

When NBA Hall of Famer Kareem Abdul-Jabbar's first money manager—a Wall Street lawyer with a conservative investment philosophy—died, Kareem turned to Tom Collins to be his sports agent, business manager and investment adviser. Collins was supposed to take care of everything.

Six years later, in 1986, Kareem severed his relationship with Collins. In those six years, Collins had taken out more than $9 million in loans in Kareem's name, had used Kareem's money to pay other clients, and had made risky investments that Kareem did not know about.

Kareem made two mistakes highlighted in the previous chapter. He signed an agreement giving Collins full power of attorney, and he ignored early signs of trouble. For example, Collins never provided the monthly statements to Kareem that their agreement required. When the first statement did not appear, red lights should have flashed. Then, Kareem received notice from the IRS that his taxes had not been paid for two years. Alarm bells!

By the time Kareem became aware of all of his losses (through an audit) and sued, it was too late. The money was gone.

Kareem now oversees his advisers and personally signs his checks. In an interview with *Sports Illustrated*, he said, "It's been a crash course in business school and I've paid a steep tuition."

"He was a good guy"

Early in Charles Barkley's basketball career, he was referred to as "The Round Mound of Rebound." Unfortunately, Sir Charles' bank account did not swell along with his belly. Barkley selected the wrong agent and financial adviser—in his case, he hired one person to manage both functions.

> *Barkley on why he selected his first agent*
> "Lance [Luchnick] was the only agent who hadn't given me money while I was in school. When it came down to my final selection, [not offering money] worked in his favor. I thought he had been smart enough to know that I couldn't be bribed...I chose him for the worst reason anybody could choose an agent—write this down, kids—because he was a good guy."

Luchnick invested Barkley's money in speculative deals that did not pan out. Barkley lost his original investment, but his problems did not end there. As Barkley notes, "When the investment goes bad, and everyone else declares bankruptcy, they keep coming after you because you're still earning money." Luchnick declared bankruptcy and Barkley won a $5-million judgment—which is hard to collect from someone with no money.

Gone with the wind

In 2004, former NBA star Scottie Pippen sued his former financial adviser, Robert Lunn. Pippen, who reportedly lost $17 million in deals recommended by Lunn, was awarded an $11.8-million judgment against the adviser. Lunn filed for bankruptcy, and Pippen is unlikely to collect much, if anything. Pippen also sued Katten Muchin, the reputable Chicago law firm that referred him to Lunn. That suit went nowhere, and Pippen was out the attorneys' fees. It gets worse. Pippen borrowed $4.375 million to buy a private jet (to lease out when he wasn't using it). The plane was a money pit, and Pippen was sued to recover the money, which he had personally guaranteed. Pippen lost in court and lost again on appeal. He has been ordered to pay the debt holder $5.021 million in principal, interest and attorneys' fees.

Agent churns former teammate

When defensive lineman Sean Jones played in the NFL, he was considered a great "locker room guy" and became the team's player representative. On retiring, Jones became a sports agent. Chris Dishman, Jones' former team-mate on the Oilers, became one of his clients. Dishman made the mistake of allowing Jones to manage his investments in addition to negotiating his playing contract. Dishman alleged that Jones engaged in unauthorized trading and in "churning" (overtrading to obtain commissions) his account. The National Assn. of Securities Dealers awarded Dishman $550,000 in damages. Dishman didn't collect any money from the judgment. Said Dishman, "It got too expensive to keep trying to track [Jones] down. I didn't have the money to keep fighting it. I didn't win anything."

Jones was also de-certified as an agent by the NFL Players Assn., meaning that he could no longer represent NFL players. The NFLPA found that Jones had violated agent regulations related to his financial dealings with Dallas Cowboy Ebenezer Ekuban. Jones persuaded Ekuban to guarantee a $1-million real estate loan that ultimately defaulted and to lend Jones $300,000, some of which was never repaid. Ekuban had to file for Chapter 11 bankruptcy protection.

Friends don't let friends rip them off

In 2002, former Washington Redskins tight end Terry Orr was sentenced to 14 months in prison for defrauding a Georgia businessman and three former Redskin teammates, including Art Monk, one of the NFL's greatest wide receivers. Each of the players invested $50,000 in Orr's shoe company, which failed. Prosecutors say Orr diverted most of the money to pay personal debts.

Financial adviser gambling heavily? It's a bad sign

Donald Lukens lived large, including dropping a lot of chips on Las Vegas blackjack tables. In 2001, the Orange County (Calif.) based financial adviser filed for bankruptcy, listing $47 million in debts and less than $1 million in assets. Lukens owed Hall of Famer Eric Dickerson $1.835 million, Carolina Panthers player Sean Gilbert $350,000, former Denver Bronco Steve Atwater $1.2 million, and Baltimore Raven Shannon Sharpe $300,000. The SEC accused Lukens of defrauding investors out of at least $25 million, and permanently barred him from the financial industry.

Let's hope "U can't touch this"

Athletes and entertainers also lose money the old-fashioned way: by spending it foolishly.

In the late 1980s and early 1990s, MC Hammer was one of the world's hottest rap stars. Yet he reportedly squandered $33 million and had to file for bankruptcy.

Hammer spent $12 million to build a house in middle-class Fremont, Calif. He hired friends and family members as contractors and builders. The "money pit from Hell" had major structural problems, and Fremont is near an earthquake fault.

Among the 11,000-square-foot house's features:
- 17 bedrooms
- recording studio
- 33-seat theater
- $2 million of Italian marble floors
- waterfalls, ponds and aquariums
- indoor and outdoor swimming pools
- tennis courts
- baseball diamond
- basketball courts
- bowling alley
- 17-car garage
- 2 gold-plated security gates with "Hammertime" signs

Other extravagant spending:
- fleet of 17 automobiles, including a Lamborghini and stretch limousine
- 2 helicopters
- $1 million in Thoroughbred racehorses
- entourage of more than 200, most of whom were on Hammer's payroll (costing $500,000 in monthly wages)
- leased Boeing 727

In April 1996, Hammer filed for bankruptcy. He reported $13.7 million in debt and $9.6 million in assets. Hammer's flawed house sold for just $5 million!

Hammer said he felt responsible for the financial support of his family and friends, but realized that in the end his family and friends did not benefit from the short-term fling.

Your friends and family may not be attuned to economic reality. Helping them grasp it may involve difficult, sensitive conversations. Such conversations go easier when you are practicing financial restraint yourself.

The never-ending list

Stories of this sort could fill a book.

Sports agent Tank Black was convicted in 2002 of stealing at least $12 million from several professional athlete clients.

Financial adviser John Gillette pled guilty in 1997 to 38 counts of grand theft and forgery. He stole at least $11 million from professional athlete clients. He touts "the Lord" as his clients' savior, but seems to favor strip clubs and casinos as his.

NFLPA executive director Gene Upshaw believes that the reported cases are just "the tip of the iceberg." He adds, "There are many cases out there where players are too embarrassed to report the fraud."

Part Four

MONEY MATTERS

SEE KID, FIRST YOU HAVE TO MAKE A
HUGE PILE OF MONEY, *THEN* YOU CAN
PLAY FOR THE LOVE OF THE GAME.

THE ROAD TO RICHES AND HAPPINESS

Neither a borrower nor a lender be/For loan oft loseth both itself and friend.
—Shakespeare's Hamlet

Chapter highlights
- Save early, save often.
- Elect (or don't opt out of) maximum 401 (k) contributions.

Savings versus spending can be a battle between David and Goliath. Unfortunately, David is a faraway, unglamorous notion that you should forgo spending in order to save for retirement, pitted against Goliath, the diabolical partnership between your desire to have everything now and a multi-billion-dollar consumer machine that works to make sure you're gratified—instantly.

Compound returns: It's magic

Those who save now—and save often—can be set for life. Studies have shown that the single biggest factor in achieving financial security is starting to invest at an early age. In his book *The Random Walk Guide to Investing*, Burton Malkiel gives an example of twin brothers who invest in Individual Retirement Accounts (IRAs). William deposits $2,000 a year for 20 years, starting at age 20, then stops, but leaves the money in the account. James starts the year William stops, and puts in $2,000 a year for 25 years, at the end of which both brothers are 65 years old. Assuming a return of 10% every year, William, who invested a total of $40,000, has almost $1.25 million at age 65. James, who invested a total of $50,000, 25% more than his brother, has less than $200,000. As you can see from this example, when gains are reinvested, time is your greatest ally. Albert Einstein once described compound interest as the "greatest mathematical discovery of all time." If you reinvest your returns, every dollar you save today (assuming an annual return of about 8.5% and investment in a tax-sheltered account) will be worth roughly $2 in eight years, $4 in 16 years, $8 in 24 years—and $64 in 48 years. (And you may need every penny of the increase to keep up with inflation.) As a pro athlete, you can be like William. You have an opportunity to save substantial amounts, then wait patiently for the magic to work.

Living—and not saving—in America

The Commerce Department reported in August 2005 that the U.S. personal savings rate had fallen to zero, and that Americans were on track to record a savings rate for the year of less than 1%—the lowest savings rate since the Great Depression of the 1930s, when most people were worried about having enough money to eat and pay the rent. In other words, lots of Americans are spending every penny they make—or more pennies than they make, by racking up credit-card debt or taking out home equity loans and auto loans. (In China, by contrast, the savings rate is reportedly 45%.)

You knew how to get by in college

When it comes to the business side of professional sports, I would say just keep the college mentality. You knew how to get by and survive when you didn't have much money. When you start earning a nice salary, you don't need to prove you have money. You can buy a few toys, like cars and electronics, but those things lose value. Invest for stability. Don't get caught up in the latest investment craze. Be smart. Make sacrifices.
—Tyus Edney, professional basketball player

Saving 101 for Athletes: The Rule of 10

In our society, few people other than professional athletes and very successful entertainers can earn millions of dollars a year while still in their 20s (or any other time for that matter). You have the opportunity to do so—and to be set for life.

Since the average career of a pro athlete lasts 4.5 years instead of the 45 years of most other professions, think of each year you play as the equivalent of 10 non-athlete work years. Base your spending on what you reasonably need to live on, not how much you currently make, knowing that your prime earning years will soon end.

As a pro athlete you have many advantages when it comes to *not spending money*. When you're on the road or in training camp, the team covers your room and board. Lots of car dealers, restaurants, clothing stores and other venders will give you discounts or freebies so that people will associate you with their products. But there are still plenty of opportunities to buy, buy, buy.

In an ideal world, I advise professional athletes to follow "The Rule of 10." Try to live on approximately 10% of your disposable income (after agent fees), and invest the rest. Depending on taxes in the state you live in, your savings rate will be 40-45%.

There are exceptions that might reasonably cause you to spend money in excess of the Rule of 10 guideline:

➤ You have credit card debt, which should be paid off as quickly as possible.
➤ Paying off credit cards is a great "investment" since the interest rates are typically far higher than the return you could get by investing the money you owe.
➤ Loved ones are in legitimate need of money. If your mother needs medical care, pay for it.
➤ You make less than $500,000. You really could live on $50,000, but spending 20% of the first $500,000 is more realistic.

There have been athletes who have made more than $50 million, even $100 million, during their pro careers, but spent so much that they ended up broke or in debt. Apply The Rule of 10, and even if your pro career is relatively short, you'll start the next phase of your life in great financial shape. If you are fortunate enough to have a long and prosperous pro career, your 10% to spend might be $600,000 or even $1 million a year—and between savings and return on investment, you might have $20 million or more in your "the-rest-of-my-life account." Even a modest 5% annual return on $20 million would give you $1 million a year to live on, even if you never worked another day in your life.

Be able to do what you want

My #1 goal for professional athlete clients is that they have enough financial security at the end of a professional sports career. Playing professional sports can provide a head start that allows athletes to transition into their next career phase without any change in lifestyle. Also, the financial benefits can allow athletes to pursue career choices without concern for meeting fixed financial obligations. That allows him to do what he *wants* to do, rather than what he *has* to do.
—Jack Mills, football agent

Million-dollar houses = million-dollar lifestyles

In the high living world of pro sports, applying The Rule of 10 is sensible, but hard. In an ESPN—The Magazine article, former Cincinnati Bengal Tim McGee refers to a financial adviser's comment, "It's the athlete in the locker room who has the worst spending habits who sets the bar for everybody else." Some of your teammates may be earning five or 10 times more than you. I know it's tough to resist the temptation to have the same cars, jewelry, clothes and luxury housing that they have. But once people catch on that your approach to spending and saving is based on a long-range outlook, you might end up with far more respect than you could get from buzzing around town in a Ferrari.

Rookies who have never owned big-ticket items are often tripped up by their actual cost. A $75,000 car costs $75,000—plus sales tax, insurance (much more insurance than you'd pay for a $30,000 car), garaging (you're not going to park it on the street), maintenance, repairs (fenders on 75K cars cost more than fenders on 30K cars) and registration fees (based on the cost of the vehicle). And the expenses associated with a car are nothing compared to those associated with an expensive house. Annual mortgage interest, real estate taxes, insurance and maintenance may come to hundreds of thousands of dollars, and that's before you have to fix the roof or a busted water pipe. **When you buy a million-dollar house, you also buy a million-dollar lifestyle.**

Tax-deductible and tax-deferred savings

The United States tax code rewards savers and investors in a number of ways. For example, there are individual retirement accounts (IRAs) and 401(k)s and other retirement accounts into which you can deposit money you've earned without paying income taxes on those earnings. On "traditional" IRAs and 401(k)s, you do not pay taxes on interest, dividends or capital gains generated by assets held in these accounts until you start making withdrawals. In recent years, Congress authorized "Roth IRA" and 401(k) accounts that are funded with after-tax dollars. You do pay income taxes on contributions to Roth accounts, but after that you don't pay any more taxes, even when you retire and withdraw the money. The tax code also rewards investing in stocks by taxing long-term capital gains and most dividends at lower rates than salaries. It encourages real estate investment by allowing improvements to be depreciated and interest to be expensed. Chapter 15 has more information on taxes.

Individual retirement accounts (IRAs)

Professional athletes generally have earnings too high to qualify for tax-deductible IRA contributions. However, you can gift money to your family and/or friends that they can contribute to their IRAs. Encouraging family members to save toward their retirement, and supporting their efforts, is one of the best uses you can make of your money and influence. An IRA might not be as exciting as a BMW, but at age 62, long after the BMW is in the junkyard, a person can retire on an IRA.

401(k)s: Believe this hype!

Your league provides a 401(k) retirement plan. Participation in the 401(k) is voluntary. You contribute to it (through a deduction from your paycheck) up to the maximum allowed by the federal government ($15,000 in 2007). Now comes the amazing part. Your professional league matches your contribution, dollar for dollar, up to a specified limit. That's a guaranteed 100% return on your money. If you are in the NFL, there is an even more amazing part. The NFL puts in $2 for each $1 of the first $10,000 you contribute. If you contribute the $15,000 maximum, the NFL adds $20,000. In the NBA, teams match 140% of the players' allowed contribution. If a player puts in $15,000, the NBA team contributes $21,000. You should *love this game.*

If you play in the NFL for five years and contribute $10,000 of your own money annually to your 401 (k), assuming a reasonable rate of return of 8%, you will have $2,884,661 when you turn 62. If you contribute the maximum $15,000, you would amass $3,365,438. That's assuming you never make another 401(k) contribution after you're 27-28 years old. If you play 10 years and contribute to the max, you will amass approximately $5,624,344.

Should you take advantage of your league's matching funds by participating in your 401 (k) and contributing the maximum every year? Or should you tell the league, "No thanks, keep your matching funds, I don't want a guaranteed 100% return." Hint: You do not need to consult a sophisticated financial expert to answer that question.

Tell your team, your agent, your financial adviser: I want to contribute to my 401(k) to the max. If you're not currently maxing your 401 (k) contribution, get on the phone. Now.

Among the many forms you will fill out when you join your team is one to enroll in your league's 401(k) plan. (The NBA recently made participation in their 401(k) a "negative election," meaning players have to opt out rather than opt in. Don't opt out.) You fill in the maximum contribution, select the funds you want to invest in, and you are on your way toward amassing the magic number of dollars you need to fund your retirement. Even if you are not ready to select funds when you fill out this form, join the plan and select the maximum contribution. Remember, your contribution is going to be matched at least dollar for dollar.

Does it seem as though participation in the 401(k) is a no-brainer? As of 2006, only 84% of the players in the NFL were taking advantage of the 2-to-1 match, and not all of them were participating to the max.

Pension plans

Unlike 401(k)s, you don't have to elect to participate in your league's pension plan or select investment vehicles. If you meet the requirements of the plan, you are automatically enrolled, and the league is required to pay you a fixed monthly or annual amount once you reach a certain age. Some of the pension plans offer an option of taking smaller payments at an earlier age, and others might do so in the future. Unless you are in dire need or don't expect to live long, it's almost always a better bet to wait until you qualify for the higher benefits. Here are the details of the league pension plans:

NBA

Eligibility Players credited with at least three seasons' experience (four years until 1993).
Fine print: League pays at least $385 per month per season played. For example: A player with six years' experience would receive $2,310 per month. Players can take a lump sum payment at age 50 or receive monthly benefits beginning at age 62.

NFL

Eligibility Players credited with at least three seasons' experience.
Benefits: $425 per month per season played. Players must be at least 55 to collect full benefits.

MLB

Eligibility Players credited with at least 43 days' experience.
Benefits: Benefits are based on experience. Base level is $34,000 per year. Players are eligible for partial benefits at age 45, full benefits at age 65.

NHL

Eligibility Players credited with at least 160 games.
Benefits: Players with fewer than 400 games' experience receive $8,000 a year after they turn 45. Players with more experience receive $12,500 per year, and a lump sum of $250,000 at age 55.

Retirement summary

Participate to the max in whatever plans are offered, for four reasons:

1. It keeps you from spending the money now.
2. Interest compounds and/or your capital appreciates.
3. Retirement accounts receive favorable tax treatment.
4. You don't pay a percentage to your agent on matching contributions from your league.

Should you share with family and friends?

Professional athletes get pulled in many directions. Issues related to family, friends, girlfriends and business can be complicated enough. Then add relatively large sums of money to the mix. You may feel an obligation to help your parents, grandparents, siblings, aunts, uncles, long-lost cousins, friends and on and on. Or they may come right out and ask for your help.

There's no right or wrong answer when it comes to providing financial support. Wanting to help is only natural—some of these people are the ones who supported you emotionally, if not financially, from the very beginning; they paid for your equipment and travel, they drove you to practices at ungodly hours, and they came to your games, rain or shine. And your inner circle of friends helped you enjoy life beyond sports. They also helped you stay grounded.

If you're not comfortable turning down a particular request, have your agent or financial adviser be the bad guy. They want to protect their client's money, and should be good at gracefully saying no.

"Neither a borrower nor a lender be"

I've stopped loaning money to family and friends. I came to the conclusion that I could never give enough. They just keep asking for more. Or they make promises they don't keep. One time I loaned a close friend a substantial amount of money based on his assurance that he would pay me back, but ultimately never did. Now when I give money, I say "I am doing so without any strings attached. It's not a loan. If you want to pay it back, great, but I am not going to sweat it." Instead of loaning thousands of dollars, I might give someone a few hundred dollars, depending on the situation. It's much easier this way. And if they ask for money to start a business, I tell them to send my financial adviser a written business plan. That weeds out a lot of financial requests.
—Anonymous NFL player

Should you pick up the check?

You go out to dinner in an expensive restaurant with a close friend you have known since elementary school. You are a millionaire. He is not. Chances are you are going to feel like picking up the check. It's a delicate situation. Your friend may offer to pay his or her share, and be relieved when you say no. Or maybe your friend will ask to leave the tip and want you to go along with that, so there is a feeling of contributing and not freeloading.

Financial disparity can cause problems in ongoing relationships with family members and friends. Feelings of guilt can drive you to pay too much, which in turn can lead to feelings of resentment, particularly when people take your money for granted, express no appreciation, and/or never offer to contribute. And there is a big difference between helping out people you've been close to forever, and being hit on by people who have recently come around, perhaps because you are wealthy.

The greatest rich friend of all time

Entourages have been around longer than the HBO show. It makes sense for athletes and entertainers to surround themselves with friends and family, within reasonable boundaries and limits. Probably the most famous athlete entourage was the one surrounding Muhammad Ali, which was well-documented in *Muhammad Ali: His Life and Times*, by Thomas Hauser.

Gene Dibble (an investment adviser to Ali in the 1970s): "There's very few of [Ali's entourage] that didn't steal from Ali in one way or another. Most of them didn't start out wanting to hurt Ali; he'd give them the money, and then they'd send the receipt to Chicago to be paid a second time. Sometimes they'd inflate the receipt too…Ali just didn't want to deal with it. I'd bring it all to his attention, but he refused to confront anybody on unpleasant matters, so they stole from him like crazy."

Maryum Ali (Ali's daughter): "My father is incredibly trusting. He's always had a blind belief in people, and he lets people get close to him who shouldn't be allowed in…My father is stubborn. You can argue with him. You can say, 'I don't trust this person for these reasons.' But in the end, he's going to trust who he wants to trust, and who he trusts is most of the world."

INVESTING 101

There are two times in a man's life when he should not speculate—
when he cannot afford it, and when he can.
—Mark Twain

Chapter highlights

- Learn the different investment vehicles available and their risk characteristics.
- Diversification and patience pay off.
- Work with investment pros, not sales pros.

Defense versus offense

Investing is like sports. Often a strong defense is more important than a high-powered offense. It's great to have your investments grow, but the single most important investment-related consideration for a professional athlete is *not to lose the money you invest.* You've worked hard to reach the pro ranks, you may never make this much money again, and you don't know how long your career will last. You do not need to take big risks. While there are no guarantees, no "sure things" or "guaranteed winners," if you follow the advice in this chapter you will make wise decisions that are likely to result in safe investments with consistent, solid returns.

So what do you invest in?

You could stuff the money you are saving into your mattress, but it would probably make for uncomfortable sleeping. A safe-deposit box at your bank would be safer and seem to involve no risk. But wait. What about the risk of inflation?

Inflation I mentioned earlier that inflation in the United States has historically averaged about 3% a year. If inflation continues at that rate, you have to make 3% on your assets each year just to stay even in terms of buying power. What are the alternatives to locking your money up in a safe-deposit box? We'll list them, starting from what are generally considered to be the most conservative (least risky) classes of investment to the least conservative (most risky).

Cash An ordinary savings account or an interest-paying checking account is appropriate for money you want to have available for spending in the next few months. Certificates of deposit, commonly called CDs, generally pay higher rates of interest and are better for money you are investing for the future. When you deposit money in a CD, you commit to keeping it there for a specified period of time, usually between three months and 10 years. Generally, the longer the commitment, the higher the interest rate. A CD in a bank that belongs to the Federal Deposit Insurance Corp. is guaranteed against bank failure for up $100,000.

Bonds A bond is a promise to pay a fixed rate of interest for a given amount of time, and then "at maturity" return the amount paid for the bond. When you buy a bond, you are essentially loaning money to the issuer of the bond. Some bonds, such as T-bills issued by the U.S. Treasury, are considered extremely conservative, low-risk investments and pay relatively low interest rates. Other bonds, including some foreign bonds and bonds issued by financially shaky corporations ("junk bonds"), are considered to be riskier investments and pay relatively higher interest rates.

Stocks Shares of stock represent partial ownership of a corporation. For example, if you own 250 shares of Nike stock, you own approximately 0.0001% (one-millionth) of the Nike Corporation, which has approximately 250 million shares of stock outstanding. Your investment grows if people are willing to pay more for a share of the stock than you did, either because the company is becoming more profitable and therefore more valuable to own, or because they think it will become more profitable in the future. Historically, the various stock market indices have increased 7 to 9% per year, but that is an average over decades. In some years, or even some years in a row, indices go down.

Real estate There are a number of ways to invest in real estate. You can buy a building (a house, apartment building, office or industrial building) and rent it, and perhaps plan to sell it eventually at a higher price than you paid. You can be part of a partnership that does the same thing. Or you can buy stock in a company that does the same, or invest in a mutual fund or exchange-traded fund (ETF) that does the same. A company that owns, manages or finances real estate may be set up as a real estate investment trust (REIT). REIT shares are traded like stocks. A REIT must distribute at least 90% of its taxable income to its shareholders annually, and can deduct dividends paid to its shareholders from its federal corporate taxable income.

Commodities Just as there are stock markets, there are commodities markets. On these markets, you can buy and sell "futures" in oil, natural gas, gold, soybeans, pork bellies, sugar and other commodities. These are bets on the future price being higher (if you bought) or lower (if you sold). Most traders never take delivery; they buy and sell contracts before the delivery date comes due.

Private deals (also known as private placements) A company founded 40 years ago has grown and generates millions of dollars of profit every year. The founders have reached retirement age, and their children are not interested in running the company. The owners, using the services of an investment banker, put the company on the market, and an investor buys it. That's a typical private deal. Often you can participate in such a deal by joining in a partnership with other investors. Investment bankers on the buying side put together such partnerships.

Venture capital Similar to private deals, but you can invest in start-up companies that are generally not yet making money, in the hopes that they will. You can put money into one deal, or into a venture capital fund that invests in many deals.

End game for private deals

Investors in private equity deals can make money in two ways: by getting a share of the profits of the company and by eventually selling the company at a higher price than they paid for it. One way of selling the company is to "go public," meaning to issue shares that investors can buy on the stock market.

All of the deals described above involve taking an ownership position in the company. Another form of private deal involves financing rather than buying. You loan money to the company or individual at a given rate of interest for a given period of time. Once the loan is repaid, the deal is over. These loans may be secured (backed by assets of the company or its owner) or unsecured. If the company fails and the loan is unsecured, you've probably lost everything except a tax write-off. If the loan is secured, you would look to the assets to recover some (or perhaps all) of your investment.

Pro athletes are frequently approached with private deals. Say your Uncle Louie wants you to invest $100,000 to help him open a restaurant. In return you will own 20% of the restaurant and get 20% of the profits. Of course a lot of things could go wrong and if there are no profits, you might lose your $100K. Investing in restaurants, nightclubs and bars, especially when they are operated by inexperienced managers, is a risky proposition.

You can buy baskets of stocks and bonds

There are a number of ways to invest in securities and real estate without having to buy individual stocks, bonds, or buildings. Here are the three most popular.

Mutual funds Through buying shares in a mutual fund you can own many different stocks or bonds with one investment. The fund, in turn, buys securities (stocks or bonds or both) with your money and the money of other investors in the fund. The value of your shares will rise and fall based on the value of the securities owned by the fund. There are many types of mutual funds. Some funds, for example, mirror the performance of the S&P 500 Index (the 500 largest U.S. public corporations) or another index. Others invest only or mainly in large cap, mid cap, or small cap stocks. ("Cap" refers to market capitalization of the company. For example, if a company has 10 million total shares and sells for $30 per share, the market cap is $30 million. This would be considered a small cap stock.) Others buy stocks in particular industries or particular countries or groups of countries.

Exchange traded funds (ETFs) Exchange traded funds, or ETFs, are like mutual funds except that you can trade them like individual stocks. There are no minimum investments, and management fees are, on average, significantly lower than for mutual funds.

Hedge funds A hedge fund is a private investment fund open only to accredited investors, currently defined as those with individual net worth over $1 million or with individual income in excess of $200,000 in each of the two most recent years. (In 2006 the SEC proposed increasing these minimums.) Hedge funds can employ all kinds of strategies: Take long (bet on a stock going up) or short (bet on a stock going down) positions; invest in stocks, options, commodities, derivatives, real estate, buyouts, arbitrage; use leverage (borrow money to invest). In recent years hedge funds, as an asset class, have performed well relative to the stock market (net of fees), although a number of them have lost money or gone under. Hedge fund management typically charges 2% of assets under management plus 20% of profits (a reward for performance). In 2007, there are approximately 8,000-9,000 hedge funds, up from just 800 in 1990.

Reduce risk through diversification

We've all heard, "Don't put all your eggs in one basket." If you invest all your money in one company and something happens that significantly reduces the value of that company, you would suffer a major loss. Even if you had invested in, say, five companies, and one took a major hit, that might be more risk than you're willing to accept. Diversification—putting your eggs in a bunch of baskets—is the key to reducing risk. To work, it has to be real diversification. For example, if you own shares in 20 different companies but they are all U.S. high-tech companies, they might all lose value at the same time, as happened when the Internet bubble burst in 2000. Properly selected mutual funds, ETFs, and REITs can be a great help in building a truly diversified investment portfolio.

Time and risk

One of the best things about being a professional athlete is being able to invest large amounts of money early in life. At a time when most people are scratching to pay the rent, you have income that you can afford to invest. By starting to invest at an early age, you have made it possible to accumulate a fortune without taking high risks. A modest return of 5 to 8% above inflation, over a period of decades, will put you in the position we talked about of being able to spend more each year of your life. You could make riskier investments that, in some years, would produce higher returns, say, 20% or even more. But if you go that route, brace yourself for similar losses. It takes several years of average returns to make up for one bad year.

Watch the fees

Mutual funds, ETFs and REITs charge annual management fees and, in many cases, other fees as well. The management fee is a percentage of the value of your investment. Money managers also charge an annual management fee. Many "financial products" such as annuities and life insurance are among the most fee-loaded investments; they should therefore be scrutinized intensely and avoided if they seem inappropriate or inferior to other possible investments. Some real estate deals are also laden with fees. In considering an investment or a money manager, it's critical to pay attention to the fees. If you get consistent excellent performance in return for the fee, it's worth it. Selecting a fund or a manager based only on low fees would make as much sense as selecting a low-cost knee surgeon. The point is to:

➤ Know what the fees are (all of them)
➤ Know what you are getting in return
➤ Not pay extravagant fees

When hiring a money manager, you have every right to ask for full disclosure of all fees, and the manager is required by law to provide you with full disclosure.

Getting started: the Zero to $5-Million Strategy

I suggest that your first goal should be to accumulate $5 million using a diversified portfolio of low-risk and low-cost investments. After that, you can consider allocating a portion of your portfolio to higher risk investments with the potential for higher return. (If done properly, these higher-risk investments can actually lower the overall risk of your portfolio.) At a modest rate of return of just 4%, $5 million produces $200,000 per year without depleting principal. Most families would love to make this much money every year, particularly without having to work. By saving and investing enough to reach the $5-million level, you guarantee a comfortable living for the rest of your life.

To employ this Zero to $5-Million Strategy

1. Avoid unscrupulous or incompetent advisers. Bad financial advisers are among the biggest dangers faced by newly minted professional athletes. College campuses are teeming with financial advisers trying to sign future pro athletes as clients. I suspect that most of the first wave of financial advisers soliciting your business will get you worse results —some far worse— than the time-tested, low-cost strategy I suggest. Of course, there are exceptions, but they are hard to identify before the fact.
2. Avoid high-risk propositions. Even ethical advisers can put clients in bad deals that come undone by market cycles.
3. Control what you can control: fees and allocation. When fees are higher than necessary, they have an ongoing negative effect on your return (the opposite effect of compound interest). Select low-fee mutual funds or ETFs based on indexes.
4. Get smart. Use the time it takes to acquire $5 million to increase your investment knowledge.

For a professional athlete just starting out, the goal should be to find slow, steady investment returns, not pie-in-the-sky schemes. Low cost index, mutual, and exchange-traded funds can be great investments, and using them reduces the likelihood of getting hooked up with a swindler.

Building greater wealth: The $5-Million and Above Strategy

Much like a building, an investment portfolio starts with a foundation. The stronger and more stable the foundation (or base), the higher you can safely build. Conversely, if the foundation is weak, the building can easily topple in a storm, flood or earthquake. With a strong foundation, your portfolio can withstand the financial equivalent of natural disasters, such as recessions, inflations and wars.

I've already talked about basing the first $5 million in your portfolio on a well-diversified group of index funds. That's one way to build a strong foundation. Once you have accumulated more than $5 million, it's reasonable to put a portion of your capital into investments that, while they can be riskier, can also yield a higher rate of return. Not only that, they can make your overall portfolio less risky by introducing more diversity. This is especially true of investments that tend to move differently than (have a low degree of correlation with) other holdings in your portfolio.

Hopefully, in the course of reaching the $5-million plateau, you have gained financial sophistication and developed relationships with reliable, accountable and expert financial professionals who can serve as your guide to these potentially more lucrative asset classes. You'll know what questions to ask and, even more important, whom to ask.

Having accumulated liquid capital of $5 million or more also gives you access to investments not available to the general public. For example, many hedge funds, private equity deals and real estate partnerships require minimum investments of hundreds of thousands of dollars, or even millions, and are out of reach for most investors.

Wanted: pro athletes

Have you ever seen a want ad or a mass mailing from an NFL, NBA or MLB team seeking players? Of course not. The athlete must develop the product (his skills, strength, endurance and so on) and market it (through performance in college or another venue) to attract the attention of pro teams, not the other way around.

Pro teams don't need advertisements and salespeople to recruit players because elite athletes know that playing in the big leagues provides an outstanding return on their investment of time, effort and sweat. In fact, it's the athletes who hire agents to help them sell themselves to teams. Similarly, the best financial deals don't need to advertise and sell; investors and their representatives seek them out.

Once you have amassed enough capital to profit from playing in this arena, you absolutely have to work with top-level advisers. As a pro athlete, you are certainly not going to have the time to screen dozens or even hundreds of private equity deals, real estate partnerships or hedge funds to find the few that have the best ratio of risk to return. Nor is it likely that you will have put in the years studying business and finance and gaining business experience that would qualify you to perform this screening even if you did have the time.

Money makes money

You've no doubt heard that "the rich get richer and the poor get poorer." There are many reasons why the rich—at least those who don't squander their money—do better than the average investor. The average investor is essentially a retail consumer who chooses from among the thousands of "products" on the shelves of the equities market. This investor pays whatever the share price is at that moment, and pays the scheduled commissions and fees. Even many wealthy investors never escape from this mindset, and as a result don't benefit from their power to individually or collectively with other wealthy investors, affect the terms and conditions of their investments. The wealthy and smart investor, however, can benefit in many ways that add up over the years. For example:

➤ By taking advantage of lower management fees typically charged to investors in certain funds or deals who put in significantly more than the minimum required.

➤ By working with a money management firm that assembles large amounts of capital and conducts due diligence thoroughly but quickly, enabling participation in deals with far better terms and conditions than those known to the average investor.

➤ By selecting, with professional help, those hedge funds that are most likely to generate high return as well as balance overall portfolio risk.

Work with a pro

This chapter introduced general ideas on how to invest. But unless you are passionate about selecting investments, have studied the subject extensively, and intend to consistently commit time to monitoring your investments and reviewing potentially better alternatives, you should work with an investment professional.

I recommend that you select a "fee-only" money manager: one that charges an annual fee based on a percentage of your assets under management, but does not get commissions, referral fees, finder's fees or any other form of compensation based on investing your money in particular financial vehicles. A fee-only manager should provide objective advice based only on the desire to grow your portfolio, which means more money for you and the manager.

I KNOW WE NEED TO GET A FIRST DOWN, BUT I'M THINKING *LONG TERM*. WHAT ARE YOU DOING TO SAVE FOR RETIREMENT?

14

INSURANCE: PLAYING THE ODDS

*I detest life-insurance agents; they always argue
that I shall some day die, which is not so.*
—Stephen Leacock, author and humorist

Chapter highlights

- The right insurance is key to protecting you, your family and your assets.
- Insurance products that may not be appropriate for you are heavily marketed by agents.
- Consult an expert who can provide objective counsel.

Life is a risk. You want to live life to its fullest, not knowing what tomorrow will bring, but you want to hedge your bets just in case something bad happens. You can't necessarily predict the future, but you can defend yourself against potential financial disasters by purchasing various types of insurance.

Everyone needs insurance. You can't drive (legally) without auto insurance. You can't participate in intercollegiate athletics without health insurance. If you're supporting a family, you want to *insure* that your loved ones will be taken care of if you die or become disabled.

The concept of insurance is basically to ask: What unfortunate things can happen to me or my businesses and my family? And how much money would be required to make me and/or my family whole? Insurance provides relief in the event something bad happens.

Some (not all) insurance agents sell their products by basically scaring the *bejesus* out of you.

What if you drop dead? Break your leg? Become paralyzed? Get into a car accident? Or what if your house burns down? Or someone slips and falls at your house and believes the cause is your negligence? Or what if your house burns down? Or someone slips and falls at your house and believes the cause is your negligence?

Instead of absorbing various losses by yourself, an insurance policy allows you to become part of a larger pool that pays off should a specified event occur. Better to pay a manageable amount (the premium) on a continuous basis than suffer two simultaneous losses: the event itself and the related costs.

Disability insurance as a pro athlete

Once you have become a professional athlete, you still might consider insuring yourself against the possibility of a career-ending injury.

Factors to consider include the following:

Percentage of your contract that is guaranteed
A guaranteed contract is basically its own insurance policy. You will be paid unless you are injured as a result of participating in dangerous, prohibited activities. In fact, to fund these guarantees, teams often take out their own insurance against players under contract becoming unable to play due to injuries.

Net worth
As a general rule, the more money you have in the bank, and the lower your annual living expenses, the less insurance you need. For example, if you have $10,000,000 in the bank (or in other liquid assets) and you and your family can live comfortably on $400,000 a year, rather than paying premiums to an insurance company, you could decide to invest the same amount of money. When you self-insure in this way, if you do not become disabled, you still have the "premiums" you paid to yourself, plus all the returns they generated.

Number of years left on your playing contracts
If you are in the final year of a contract, you might turn down a long-term deal from your current team in order to wait for free agency. In this situation, you could take out a larger insurance policy for 12 months to protect yourself while you're playing under a short-term, perhaps below-market deal.

Property and liability insurance

Every tangible asset (cars, boats, real estate) you own must be insured.

Professional athletes are targets for lawsuits, many of which are frivolous. People often sue those with "deep pockets." If a pro athlete is in the vicinity when someone claims to have suffered an injury or loss, even if there are many others present and the athlete had little or nothing to do with it, odds are he will be sued. Therefore you need to protect your assets with sufficient liability insurance, available through homeowners' and auto policies, and also through an "umbrella policy." Having sufficient liability insurance also saves you the expense associated with hiring lawyers to represent you. The insurance company generally takes care of the legal defense.

Life insurance

If family members depend on you financially, you will want to provide for them in the event of your death. If your estate is large enough, and you have made a proper will, that should be sufficient. But if you are not leaving enough to support their lifestyle, education, health expenses and so on, you will want to purchase life insurance. Or, in consultation with your financial adviser, you might conclude that insurance would be a good way to pay your estate tax, if any.

There are two broad categories of life insurance: term and whole life. I suggest that you buy term life insurance, where you pay and (in most cases) are insured for a given number of years, such as five or 10. Whole life policies are investment vehicles as well as life insurance policies. They cost far more than term policies and are generally not considered to be good investments compared to well-selected stocks and bonds.

Annual review

Once you've purchased insurance, don't just sit on it. As your situation changes, you may need to adjust your coverage. Let's hope that over time you have more assets to protect. And your family situation may change. An annual review will prevent you from cruising along with holes in your coverage, with too little coverage or with too much (and therefore with unnecessarily high premiums), or with the wrong beneficiaries.

Final word

When it comes to purchasing any type of insurance, consult an expert who can provide objective counsel. The amount of insurance you buy should be based on the probability of a negative event (such as fire, flood, earthquake, death) versus the premium costs, not emotion or fear induced by high-pressure insurance agents.

HE WON'T LEAVE UNTIL MY TAXES ARE PAID!

TAXES AND ESTATE PLANNING BASICS

*I want to find out who this FICA guy is and
how come he takes so much of my money.*
—Nick Kypreos, NHL player, at Detroit Red Wings'
2004 White House ceremony

Chapter highlights

- Aim to minimize, not evade, your taxes.
- If you claim residency in a state with low (or no) income tax, act like you live there.
- Work with a tax expert.

This chapter provides a broad overview of estate planning. You can use it as a general guide when you seek professional tax advice. The details and nuances of tax and estate planning are too numerous and complex to cover here.

You are legally required to file a federal income tax return every year. You are also required to report every dollar you earn, from every source. You also have to file state tax returns for each state in which you played that has an income tax, and in the state where you live if it has an income tax.

Your salary is likely to put you in the top tax bracket, which means you will pay 35% of it to the federal government (not including your payment into Social Security), and up to another 9.3% in state income tax (state income tax rates vary from zero to 9.3%). In some municipalities, such as New York City, there is an additional local income tax (generally collected by the state through state income tax returns).

Taxes will be deducted from your paycheck. When you file your tax return, you will be requesting a refund or paying more, depending on your other income (interest and dividends, endorsements, employment during the off season, and so on), taxes (if any) paid on your other income, and deductions you may qualify for, such as dependents, medical expenses, mortgage interest, investment losses (if any), and many others.

Clearly, taxes are going to take a huge bite out of your hard-earned income. Depending on your feelings about how the government is spending your money, you may think this is a good deal or a rip-off. Regardless, your goal should be to minimize taxes, not evade them.

Why not cheat?

No matter how you feel about your obligation to pay taxes, it is illegal to not file a federal tax return and also to not pay your taxes.

Tax evasion is one of the few crimes you can commit by doing nothing—for example, by neglecting to file a tax return. If the Internal Revenue Service (IRS) suspects that you are not paying what you should, they will conduct an audit. Just preparing for an audit, which can involve the services of an accountant, bookkeeper and lawyer, can cost a lot of money. If the IRS finds that you have indeed paid too little, you will be required to pay what you owe, plus interest and substantial penalties. If they find, in addition, that you have committed outright fraud (for example, by claiming a bogus tax deduction or hiding income offshore), you can even be charged with a crime, tried and, if convicted, fined and/or sent to jail (to say nothing of the effect on your athletic career, endorsements and future employment).

Many people evade taxes and don't get caught, or at least don't get caught for a long time. A pro athlete is probably more likely to be caught than most people, because as a high earner he's a good target for the IRS (if they go to the expense of auditing someone, they want to recover lots of money), and as someone with a high profile, he's an even better target. Publicity around his or her case could impress Joe Average Taxpayer with the need to pay taxes.

You have no choice about reporting the income from your salary—your team reports it to the government on a Form W-2 (and deducts money and sends it to federal and state governments). Savings and investment institutions report interest, dividends and capital gains to the government, but generally do not deduct taxes.

A pro athlete is most likely to get in trouble with the IRS in the following ways:

➤ Neglecting to file taxes or missing payment deadlines.
➤ Not reporting additional income. For example, athletes can make good money signing autographs—thousands of dollars at an autograph show. And it's often paid in cash. It can be tempting not to report it (or you could

even innocently forget). A number of professional athletes—especially baseball players—have been caught failing to report income from sports memorabilia. Pete Rose was hit with a $154,000 tax bill. Hall of Famers Duke Snider and Willie McCovey pleaded guilty to tax evasion. Darryl Strawberry pleaded guilty to failing to pay taxes between 1986 and 1990.

➤ Falling for a "sophisticated tax strategy" that turns out to be illegal. The pitch, from an accountant, tax lawyer or someone claiming to be a tax expert, may sound like this: "Smart, wealthy people don't pay taxes like everybody else; they take advantage of loopholes in the constantly changing, complicated tax code. And we have discovered just such a loophole. Our fee to prepare your return is nothing compared to what you will save." By the time the IRS comes around (there is a three-year statute of limitations to audit your tax filing, but no statute of limitations if fraud is involved), the firm you hired may be long gone and you are on your own. If it sounds too good to be true, it probably is.

Paying is not enough

If the IRS audits your tax return, the burden of proof is on you, not them. If they question a deduction, you have to prove that you were entitled to it. Therefore, in addition to paying your taxes, keep records that document the amounts you deduct on your return. Assuming you are relying on an accountant or tax preparer, be sure that they are keeping such records. You can minimize the paperwork by always paying by check or credit card.

Minimize taxes

You have to pay your taxes. But you do not have to overpay. Avoiding overpaying is not simple. The tax code is complicated. You want an accountant who will take advantage of every deduction you're entitled to, but who will not push the limits so hard that you lose sleep waiting for the auditor to knock on your door.

You spend much more time preparing for a game (practice, fitness training, studying film, planning and so on) than playing the game. Successfully minimizing taxes requires a similar approach. If the tax return is the game, tax planning is the preparation. Meet with your accountant or tax attorney to discuss the tax consequences of investments, buying or selling a house, moving, structuring a business deal, charitable contributions—anything that is likely to effect your income or deductions. (For example, it may save you money to make a transaction in December rather than January, or vice versa.)

Residency and state taxes

Where you live—or, more precisely, the state you declare as your primary residence—can have a significant effect on your after-tax income. Forty-one states, including California, Illinois, and New York, have state income taxes. Others, such as Nevada, Florida, and Washington, have none. Among the states that do have income taxes, the rate varies significantly.

The Jock Tax

You pay state taxes on your salary in the states where you play games. This is known as the "jock tax." States have the right to collect tax from nonresidents who do business there. Athletes have been targeted to pay this tax primarily because of the money involved, and because salaries of professional athletes are available to tax agencies. Most states apply a "duty days" or games-played formula to calculate the tax liability. Your accountant or tax adviser should be familiar with multi-state tax filings.

Birth of the Jock Tax

In 1991, the Chicago Bulls played the Los Angeles Lakers in the NBA Finals. The state of California decided to go after Bulls superstar Michael Jordan, because his salary was so high, for income earned in California. Today, according to a Tax Foundation report, "of the 24 states that have a professional sports team, only four do not have a jock tax."

You can say you live anywhere. But if the tax department of another state claims you actually reside in their state, you will have to prove that your primary residence is where you say it is, or you might be subject to penalties and even charged with tax fraud. If you grew up in California, a state with high income tax, and were drafted by a Florida team, it will make sense to establish residence in the Florida, a state with no income tax. Establishing Florida residency for tax purposes won't be a problem because you will spend at least six months in Florida. If you play for a team in a high-taxed state, you can buy a house in, say, zero-state-income-tax Nevada. But it's not as simple as merely claiming residency. You must be able to demonstrate that you actually reside where you say you do.

Here are some ways to support a residency claim:

- Register to vote in your state.
- Register cars with its department of motor vehicles.
- Obtain a driver's license there.
- Have your bills sent to your address there.
- Purchase property there.
- Send your children to school there.
- Put your primary bank accounts in your new state.
- Conduct business affairs there.
- Spend significant time during your off-season there.

If you want to establish a new state residency, particularly in a state that has little to no state income tax, consult with a qualified CPA to ensure that your residency is properly established.

Bottom line for filing and paying taxes

Work with a qualified tax expert. File on time. Pay on time. Err on the side of caution. Don't cheat. If it sounds too good to be true…you know the rest.

Estate planning

In sports it is often the little things that count the most. A spectacular dunk or touchdown run gets played on *SportsCenter*, but it is often a box-out by a forward or a block by an offensive lineman that make the highlight possible. Spreading good cheer through gifts to loved ones may get you immediate glory, but it is tax and estate planning that, like an anonymous offensive lineman, could be the big difference-maker.

No one wants to think about death, especially when we're young and healthy. But for people with money, proper estate planning is critical to their financial and legal affairs.

Estate planning enables your wealth to go to those you want to inherit it, in the amounts you want, and under the conditions you want (for example, in trust for children or young adults until they reach a certain age). It enables you to be sure your money goes to any charities you select, as well as to individuals. And proper estate planning (through gifts and setting up trusts, among other ways) can significantly reduce your tax burden while you are still alive.

Other benefits of estate planning

Avoid uncertainty In the worst-case scenario, you die unexpectedly without having made a will, let alone engaged in more thorough estate planning. If you have significant assets (the amount depends on your state of residence), who inherits what will be determined in a court, by a probate judge. The judge may also determine who becomes the caretaker of your children. A portion of your estate will pay the court costs and the legal fees of the lawyer the court appoints to represent your estate. If there are relatives and/or charities contending for portions of the estate, the legal fees can become enormous.

Wealthy people typically avoid having their estates go through probate by preparing (with the help of an estate and taxation lawyer) not only a will, but also a revocable living trust. The trust names trustees whom, upon your death, become responsible for distributing the assets according to your written instructions.

Minimize estate taxes In 2007, if your net worth is $2 million or more, your estate is subject to estate tax. In 2009, the minimum increases to $3.5 million and, as of now, in 2010 the estate taxes will be completely repealed. There's a good chance Congress will reinstitute the estate tax before 2010 (if not, expect a lot of people to be on life support in 2009). The more you are worth, the higher your estate taxes. Currently, the maximum estate tax is 45%! A good estate and taxation lawyer can help you minimize the tax consequences of death. Note: If you're married, your estate generally transfers to your spouse tax-free.

Provide for your children In the event of your untimely death, it is critical to provide for their care, including guardianship, education and money. If you are legally married, you may assume that this is not a problem; your wife will carry on. But what happens to your children if, for example, you are both killed in the same automobile accident?

The road to nowhere

Derrick Thomas, an All-Pro linebacker for the Kansas City Chiefs, died February 8, 2000 from injuries suffered in a car wreck. At the time of his death, Thomas had seven children from five women…and no will. In his football career, Thomas earned more than $30 million, but according to reports was worth less than $2 million when he died.

Without a will, a significant chunk of Thomas' hard-earned money ended up going to Uncle Sam and lawyers, and less to the care of his children.

Part Five

BODY AND MIND MATTERS

HEALTHY CHOICES

Going to bed with a woman never hurt a ballplayer.
It's staying up all night looking for them that does you in.
—Casey Stengel, Hall of Fame baseball manager

Chapter highlights

- On the whole, people don't make good decisions after midnight.
- Big Brother is watching.
- If you have a mental or social issue, it's almost always better to get professional help.

Being a professional athlete is a rare opportunity to play your sport at the highest level—and get paid to do what you presumably love. But like any great opportunity, being a pro athlete comes with dangers.

Some of the dangers are not under your control. Some players are blessed genetically with bodies that can withstand the physical punishment of pro sports better than others. Others see their careers end in an instant from one devastating hit or freak landing.

Preachers, teachers, human creatures

Young athletes grow accustomed to living a structured, sometimes even sheltered life. Parents, coaches, teachers, counselors and other adults constantly tell them where to go, when to be there, what to do, what not to do and how to behave. Most of this advice is dispensed during daylight hours and seems to make perfect sense. "Here's what you need to do to be successful. You know the difference between right and wrong. Do right. End of moral lesson…until next time." But what it fails to consider is, well, life.

At 3 p.m. you might be thinking rationally. Now enter the following into the human equation: music thumping, scantily clad females gyrating, alcohol flowing, hormones raging. At 2 a.m. under those conditions, it can be hard to process information clearly. Particularly if some of the alcohol has flowed into your body, the consequences of your decisions might seem inversely proportional to your invincibility, the perils insignificant, irrelevant and infinitesimal. You might not even notice an obvious danger right in front of you, such as a jealous ex-girlfriend or a drunken idiot eager to prove himself against a famous athlete. Suddenly, it's a whole different night, and you are at a crossroads. If a drunk decks you, you lose. From the point of view of your athletic career, if you deck him, you might lose more. If he pulls a knife or a gun…let's not even go there.

Once you have had a few alcoholic beverages, unless you've taken precautions in advance, you can easily decide to drive, despite the hundreds of warnings you've heard while sober. You may be stopped by the police or, far worse, kill or injure yourself or someone else. You can just as easily get into trouble without doing anything illegal, just by responding to your pulsating surroundings. It can be a woman whose motives you don't know, unprotected sex, gambling or other forms of risky behavior that could lead to negative outcomes. Either you act sensibly or you don't. Either you suppress or moderate your impulses or you increase the chances that something bad might happen.

Every indiscretion will come out

Decades ago an athlete could come across as a hero even if his private life was out of control. Today there is no such thing as a private life for a professional athlete. The media, which once all but collaborated with leagues and owners to protect the image of athletes, is now committed to exposé. Nor does the media have to rely on a handful of reporters to dig for dirt. Millions of fans equipped with cellphones, digital cameras and blogs—the so-called "snaparazzis"—are poised to snap photos of athletes when they spot them in restaurants, bars or other public places. Photos of drunk athletes fighting or embracing women other than their wives can immediately end up on a Web site. (Many diehard New England sports fans were offended when their quarterback, Tom Brady, was photographed wearing a New York Yankees hat.) Deadspin.com, withleather.com and thesmokinggun.com are but a few of the Web sites devoted to guaranteeing that every indiscretion (or seeming indiscretion) by a pro athlete (or other celebrity) is available for public consumption. Have a brush with the law and there's a good chance your mug shot, the police report and any legal documents filed will come up when you are Googled—for years to come.

Be aware of your environment. If you're out in public, you're fair game for fans and paparazzi. Nothing wrong with letting a little steam off, having a cocktail, hanging out with friends (even very attractive ones). But be mindful of how photos might look online...to your family, friends and employees.

Dangerous and undesired activities

Professional athletes are paid to play their sport. Professional sports teams are protected from having to pay when athletes are unable to play due to non-sports-related injuries. Paragraph three of the NFL standard player contract is typical. It reads: "Players will not engage in any activity other than football which may involve a significant risk of personal injury."

The NFL doesn't specifically mention motorcycle riding as a prohibited activity, but it is reasonable to assume that this activity poses significant risk, and, therefore, is prohibited. Basically, if a football player gets hurt due to something outside football, a team is within its rights under the collective bargaining agreement to recoup a portion of any signing bonus as well as withhold salary while a player is unable to perform. The NBA, NHL and MLB specifically identify dangerous activities. Paragraph 12 of the NBA uniform player contract lists a group of prohibited activities, including "the riding of motorcycles and mopeds, skiing and skydiving." So before you purchase a motorcycle or sign up for flying lessons, check with your agent or players association for clear guidance.

The latest collective bargaining agreement also gives NFL teams the right to terminate the contract of any player who has "engaged in personal conduct reasonably judged by [the] club to adversely affect or reflect on club."

Not-so-super humans

No matter how absurd the hype, it gets into our heads. Sometimes we have to remind everyone, including ourselves, that elite athletes are human beings, not the bigger-than-life superheroes they play in televised games and shoe commercials. They suffer the same psychological problems as the general population, at the same rate or perhaps even higher due to the surreal world of professional sports.

You can use this chapter to help you think about your mental state and how it affects your athletic performance, happiness and peace of mind. We live in an "Oprah" nation, where once-taboo subjects are now openly discussed (and discussed and discussed). If you have a problem, you're almost undoubtedly better off talking it over with a trustworthy friend, a mentor or an experienced mental health professional rather than keeping it bottled up inside.

Hide the problem or seek help?

Professional teams (and now even some colleges) employ former FBI agents to conduct background checks of potential team members. Before pro teams draft a player, they usually know just about everything there is to know about that player. Athletes believe, often correctly, that if any kind of problem shows up (drugs, gambling, a referral for anger management counseling), they will be downgraded in the draft. Thus they learn to hide problems rather than seek help in dealing with them.

More often than not, hiding the problem not only fails to resolve it, but also fails to keep it hidden. There are federal privacy laws that protect the confidentiality of medical records. But when a psychological problem results in the arrest of an elite athlete for DUI, assault, spousal abuse, possession of drugs or anything else, the media is on it in a flash.

Leagues and players associations, to their credit, have become more sensitive to these issues and have instituted programs to educate players and make them more comfortable seeking help.

CAN THE GENIE INTEREST YOU IN A
PERFORMANCE-ENHANCING POTION?

17

GAMBLING AND PERFORMANCE-ENHANCING DRUGS

The only way to win money in a casino is to own it.
—Steve Wynn, owner, Wynn Resorts, Las Vegas

Chapter highlights

- Follow rules and laws regarding gambling.
- Be careful about what you put into your body.
- Check with your trainer before taking any supplement or even medication to make sure it does not contain any banned or illegal substances.

Two of the biggest problems facing sports at all levels are gambling and the use of performance-enhancing drugs. Look no further than 2007: Despite its wild popularity, sports is mired by controversies involving steroids (the Tour de France and Major League Baseball, in particular) and gambling (NBA official Tim Donaghy pleaded guilty to a conspiracy to defraud the NBA by using inside information to beat the point spread). Some forms of gambling violate league rules, as does the use of just about any performance-enhancing drug. Additionally, gambling and drug use can lead to legal problems, financial problems and serious risks to physical and mental health. Therefore they can threaten an athlete's ability to earn a living in professional sports. And there are potential heath risks associated with drug use.

As a group, athletes are among the most competitive people in our society. Those who have fought hard enough and long enough to reach the pro level tend to be off-the-charts competitive. They always look for an edge, and drugs, whatever the risks of using them, can offer an edge. As for gambling, it can keep the competitive juices flowing 24 hours a day, so there's never an emotional letdown between games and practices.

Gambling: You bet your life

Gambling is so much a part of mainstream American culture today that you have no choice but to relate to it, either by participating to one degree or another or by declining to participate. Casinos are designed to seduce visitors away from everything they've learned about the value of money. To help athletes make informed decisions, Rick Rhoads and I wrote a booklet called *The Truth about Gambling, Athlete's Edition*. (It's available at www.a-game. com.) In it we showed mathematically that if you gamble at casinos, tracks, with bookies, online or by playing state lotteries, over a period of time you will lose money.

Some athletes have gambled away enormous sums of money. Golfer John Daly estimates that he has blown at least $50 million playing slot machines and blackjack. Daly and former basketball great Charles Barkley have been forthcoming about their gambling problems. They deserve credit for sharing their experiences for the benefit of others.

As an athlete you may be "Like Mike," wired to take risks

A reporter once asked Michael Jordan's father, James, "Does your son have a gambling problem?" He replied, "[Michael] doesn't have a gambling problem…What he does have is a competition problem. He was born with that. And if he didn't have a competition problem, you guys wouldn't be writing about him."

As a competitive athlete, even after losses, you're probably confident that you'll win the next time out. In sports and in life, that confidence can be a great trait. It can keep you from dwelling on defeat and motivate you to learn more about what it takes to win.

In other areas of life, however, such confidence can be a formula for disaster. It can encourage you to believe you can engage in risky behavior and always get away with it. Ultimately, however, the odds catch up to you.

League rules

If you played at an NCAA institution, you were not permitted to gamble on college or professional sports. Gambling policies of professional sports leagues are less restrictive. A player in the NFL, NBA, NHL and MLB is allowed to place legal wagers on sports events except on games in his own league. For example, an NBA player can bet on an NFL game, but not on an NBA game (whether or not his team is playing). Note, however, that the rule permits "legal wagers." In the United States, sports wagering is legal only in Nevada, and you must be physically in Nevada to place a bet. Millions of people bet on sports illegally through bookies or online, and few are prosecuted. Nevertheless, it's probably not a good idea for a highly visible professional athlete to place bets with bookies.

Leagues want to keep players, coaches and referees away from bookies to prevent even the appearance of collusion. Leagues fear that if players, coaches or referees develop relationships with bookies, they may divulge information which is not publicly available that can affect point spreads—information about injuries, for example. Even worse—the nightmare scenario—is that, finding themselves heavily in debt to bookies, they agree to shave points or otherwise affect the outcome of a game, leading to a scandal that would disenchant the public.

If you should ever find yourself unable to control your gambling, or headed in that direction, you're not alone. Studies have shown that about 5% of U.S. adults are addicted to gambling. This addiction is treatable, so you should immediately seek professional help. Of course you want your gambling problem to be kept confidential. One of the best sources of information for finding help is your players association. Another is Gamblers Anonymous: www.gamblersanonymous.org.

Performance-enhancing drugs

The following approaches are typically used to educate athletes about the dangers of steroids and other performance-enhancing drugs (I'll use "steroids" as shorthand for all of them).

Scared straight: Describe potential harmful effects of using steroids over a period of time. The list includes pain and difficulty urinating, baldness, impotence, shrunken testicles, heart disease, growth of female-like breast tissue, liver damage, cancer, even death. There are several prominent athletes whose deaths in their 30s and 40s are thought to be related to the use of anabolic steroids.

Risk analysis: Analyze the risk of not taking steroids—maybe playing slightly less effectively—against the risks of taking them—a chance of being banned by your league and of being convicted of a crime, with loss of your pro sports career and adverse effects on any other career, plus the possibility of developing health problems.

Morality: To keep the game pure, we need to root out those who jeopardize the integrity of the sport.

Presumably, if you are swayed by one or more of these arguments, you won't knowingly take steroids. But is it enough to "just say no"? What is rarely talked about is the impact of athletes who use steroids on those who don't.

Think about a course you took in which the professor graded on a curve. The breakdown might have been something like this:

A: 20%; B: 20%; C: 50%; D: 5%; F: 5%

Your grade is based not solely on your work, but on your work compared to the work of other students in the class. Professional teams "grade" athletes in a similar manner, but with salaries instead of letters. The highest-graded players get the A contracts. Then the B contracts and so on. Get an F and you're out of the league.

In the class, each student who cheats to get a higher grade pushes another student down to a lower grade. The same can happen in sports. Athletes who enhance their performance by cheating with steroids can push you down to a lower-level contract or worse. How would you feel if you were cut from a team and the last roster spot went to someone who was taking steroids?

It's in your enlightened self-interest not only to avoid steroids, but to work with your players association to get them out of the game. Professional leagues are working to root out steroid users. Players associations have the same goal, but at the same time, want to preserve athletes' privacy and prevent owners from using drug testing as a weapon against players.

A slippery slope

Congress, team owners and the media are up in arms about steroid use, and portray efforts to limit testing in highly charged, negative terms. It would be easy for players associations to give in to the pressure to randomly test athletes without any restrictions and without cause. But it would be a disservice to their members. An owner can use drug testing to rid his team of unwanted contracts. What owner wouldn't want to tear up a long-term, guaranteed contract of an unproductive player?

New magic potions

As fast as leagues ban steroids and other performance-enhancing drugs, other "magic potions" make their way into locker rooms. Be careful about taking unproved and potentially dangerous substances, even if they are not (yet) banned.

Ultimately, you are responsible for whatever goes into or onto your body, knowingly or unknowingly. Even if you are getting a massage, you need to know what is being rubbed onto your skin. Ignorance is not an excuse. Obtain a copy of your league's list of banned substances and keep it handy. Check with your trainer. Exercise common sense.

Leagues now have a supplement hotline that you can call if you are unsure about a product. The NFL and MLB have pre-approved supplements manufactured by several companies, including EAS.

Cure the common cold, get banned

In a June 28, 2006 article in *USA Today*, Seattle Seahawks quarterback Matt Hasselbeck said when he ordered a fruit smoothie, the server asked him for his choice of boost. Hasselbeck requested the "fat burner." Then he thought better. He said, "Wait a minute; I don't know what's in that stuff."

Even certain over-the-counter medications are off-limits for fear of producing a positive result. Said Hasselbeck, "I have allergies, and I can't take Claritin-D anymore, because it has Sudafed [an NFL-banned substance] in it. What I can give my 4-year-old daughter, I can't take myself."

As this book goes to press, a movement is developing to differentiate between systematic use of performance-enhancing drugs and one-time, accidental use of cold medicine, especially when the quantity is too small to have an effect on performance. But I would caution all athletes to make it a habit to read labels…especially in foreign countries. An over-the-counter medication which does not contain any banned substances in the United States is available in Europe: But there it contains ephedrine, a substance banned by most professional leagues and sports federations.

Final word

The two most obvious reasons not to use steroids are: 1) they are banned from professional sports leagues and associations, and 2) some performance-enhancing drugs are illegal. In the past, apprehending steroid manufacturers and users was a low priority by both law enforcement and sports governing bodies. That is no longer true. The BALCO case has become a dragnet for not only arguably the most sophisticated, clever steroid manufacturer ever, but also several alleged (and subsequently admitted) steroid users. As this book goes to press, it is too early to measure the ultimate fallout from the BALCO case. Additionally, in November 2007, Major League Baseball is expected to release findings from Senator George Mitchell's steroid investigation, which reportedly cost $15 million to conduct and is likely to cast another cloud over professional sports.

Players may have gained significant economic advantages by using steroids when testing and enforcement was weak. The hope is that current players will now calculate the risk/reward scenario differently: The real risks of using are now greater than any perceived benefits.

Part Six

TODAY'S BIG-DOLLAR ERA OF PROFESSIONAL SPORTS

LOOKS LIKE SOMEBODY HAD A LATE NIGHT.

THE FIGHT TO EMERGE FROM THE DARK AGES

If there is no struggle there is no progress. Those who profess to favor freedom and yet depreciate agitation…want crops without plowing up the ground, they want rain without thunder and lightning…Power concedes nothing without a demand. It never did and it never will.
—Frederick Douglas, 19th-Century abolitionist and noted author, quoted by Curt Flood in *The Way It Is*, explaining why Flood decided to challenge baseball's reserve clause

Do you know...

- Who founded your league's players association? When?
- What the "reserve clause" refers to?
- How former athletes Curt Flood, Oscar Robertson, Spencer Haywood, John Mackey, Marvin Powell, Freeman McNeil, Reggie White and Andy Messersmith helped you?
- Who Marvin Miller is and how he affected professional sports?
- The average salary in your league 20 years ago? Ten years ago? Today?

This chapter answers some of those questions. There are many Web sites, articles and books that will help you gain a deeper understanding of how pro athletes fought for the salaries and benefits that you get today. A great place to start is at the history section of your players association Web site:

NBA http://www.nbpa.com/history.php
NFL http://www.nflpa.org/AboutUs/main.asp?subPage=History
MLB http://mlbplayers.mlb.com/NASApp/mlb/pa/info/history.jsp
NHL http://www.nhlpa.com/AboutTheNHLPA/WhatIs.asp

The Dark Ages

Football In 1968, the NFL Players Assn. represented players on only 16 of the NFL's 26 teams. When players on the other 10 teams accepted a contract that kept the minimum salary at $9,000 for rookies and $10,000 for veterans, exhibition game pay at $50 per game, and pension eligibility at age 65, the NFLPA felt it had no choice but to go along.

Basketball In 1958, the average player salary in the NBA was $12,000. There was no minimum salary, no health benefits, and no pension plan. In 1954, after threatening not to play in the first televised NBA All-Star Game, the players received a per diem increase to $8 a day and a pension plan. In 1970, a group of 14 NBA players filed a class-action lawsuit that ultimately led to an agreement eliminating the reserve clause and creating free agency. The average salary jumped from $35,000 in 1970 to $200,000 in 1976.

Baseball From 1948 through 1967, due to the reserve clause, the minimum salary in baseball was $6,000. In 1968, the Major League Baseball Players Assn. negotiated the first collective bargaining agreement in professional sports. It raised the minimum salary to $10,000. In 1970, the association achieved another first when it won the right to arbitration to resolve grievances. Before that there was no legal mechanism for players to challenge owners and management.

Professional athletes as property

The reserve clause, which had been a standard part of all MLB contracts since 1876, bound a player to his team for his entire career, allowing him to be traded or sold without his approval, like a piece of property. The clause made it impossible for a player to establish his value in a free market. Lawsuits (by a team vs. a league, a minor league player, an unsigned player, and finally by major leaguer Curt Flood) claimed that the clause violated the Sherman Antitrust Act of 1890, which makes it illegal to conspire to restrain "trade or commerce among the several states." Baseball argued that it was engaged in exhibitions which the U.S. Supreme Court, in 1922 and again in 1953, agreed were "purely state affairs," and therefore not subject to the Sherman Act. Through the 1960s, baseball owners used this legal windfall to suppress salaries.

After the 1969 season, the Cardinals traded Curt Flood to the Philadelphia Phillies. Flood refused to go, sitting out the entire 1970 season and forsaking his $100,000 salary. He was challenging Major League Baseball's reserve clause. Although in Flood v. Kuhn (then-Major League Baseball commissioner Bowie Kuhn) the Supreme Court ruled against Flood, the case paved the way to what we now know as free agency. In December 1975, an independent arbitrator ruled that the reserve clause was invalid.

During Flood's trial, MLB owners and even some ballplayers testified that if the reserve clause were overturned, professional baseball would be in jeopardy. And what has happened since? Franchise values—along with player salaries—have skyrocketed. In May 2007, MLB Commissioner Bud Selig apologized for the reserve clause, saying it "should have been modified decades before someone like me came into the sport. Change was long overdue, and some balance to the relationship was necessary." Added Selig: "So much of our success has been made possible because of our improved relationship with the players."

If there were a pro athletes hall of fame, Curt Flood would be the first member

The reserve clause exists for two reasons: One, to cut down on the money the ballplayers get, and, two, to give a feeling of power to men who like to play God over other people's lives.
—Curt Flood

For most of his 15-year career in baseball, Curt Flood played for the St. Louis Cardinals. A three-time All-Star and seven-time Gold Glove winner, Flood's career batting average was .293. In 1966, appearing in 159 games, Flood went the entire season without committing an error in center field. He helped the Cardinals win the World Series in 1964 over the New York Yankees and, in 1967, over the Boston Red Sox.

Time magazine named Curt Flood one of the "10 Most Influential Sports Figures of the 20th Century," stating "[Flood] was more successful on the field than he was in court, but when outfielder Curt Flood sued baseball in 1970 to win the right to sell his services to the highest bidder, he initiated a process that would destroy the feudal structure of pro sports. Flood lost his battle; his fellow players, in time, won the war. Those who do not thank him daily in their prayers should be ashamed of themselves."

Marvin Miller, director of the MLBPA during Flood v. Kuhn, said, "At the time Curt Flood decided to challenge baseball's reserve clause, he was perhaps the sport's premier center fielder. And yet he chose to fight an injustice, knowing that even if by some miracle he won, his career as a professional player would be over. At no time did he waver in his commitment and determination. He had experienced something that was inherently unfair and was determined to right the wrong, not so much for himself, but for those who would come after him. Few praised him for this, then or now."

Professional athletes owe Curt Flood a debt of gratitude for what he did to bring them the benefits of the free market. Curt Flood belongs in the Baseball Hall of Fame for his profound and lasting contribution to the game of baseball and the business of professional sports.

Not-so-free agency

Now that players associations have dramatically changed the balance of power in professional sports, they can rest, right? Wrong. Owners have been known to long for, and try to bring back, "the good old days" of dominance over athletes. MLB owners, for example, had been angry about free agency ever since it was introduced. They felt it was responsible for taking money from their pockets and putting it into players' pockets. From 1985 to 1987, the owners colluded to refrain from bidding on free agents.

What happened? The marketplace no longer determined salaries. In 1986, Detroit Tigers pitcher Jack Morris became a free agent. He had won 21 games that year, making him a 20-game winner for the second time in four seasons. Yet he was not offered a contract by any other club. That year, because of the owners' agreement not to bid, Morris and several other players went without offers. MLBPA eventually filed a legal complaint, alleging that the owners had violated the 1981 collective bargaining agreement. The courts ruled in the players' favor and required owners to pay $280 million in damages. More important, the ruling ended the three-year run of collusion and returned free-market competition for the services of free agents.

Today some owners, especially those in smaller-market cities, still balk at paying top dollar for free-agent players, but overall the system works to preserve a free market. Anti-collusion provisions are explicitly spelled out in labor agreements, including steep financial penalties if players associations prove collusion is or was occurring.

The draft, then and now

Today, you have less of a chance of being drafted by an NBA or NFL team than you did years ago, even though leagues still need to draft the same number of players (or more with league expansion). That's because players associations have negotiated collective bargaining agreements (CBAs) reducing the number of rounds in the draft. Paradoxically, you are now better off not being drafted than being drafted in one of the former late rounds. If more than one team has an interest in acquiring a player, as an "undrafted free agent" that player has some choice as to where he plays. He may also have some bargaining leverage regarding his salary.

The NBA Draft is 2 rounds, down from 10 rounds in 1984. The NFL Draft is 7 rounds, down from 12 in 1992.

MLB's draft marathon

The first MLB amateur draft, in 1965, had three "phases." Now it has a roughly comparable 50 rounds. To feed baseball's minor leagues, approximately 1,500 players are selected each year. (There are only 750 players on MLB rosters.) While the NFL and the NBA rely on college sports (mostly NCAA schools) to yield the next crop of future pro athletes, MLB funds an elaborate farm system to develop its talent. While college baseball is an excellent training ground, almost every player does time "down on the farm."

Rival leagues

Up until the 1960s, owners had significant leverage over players. Owners worked in concert to maximize revenue and minimize expenses. Armed with the reserve clause, they had little incentive to negotiate in good faith. The only time owners had to compete for the services of players was when fledging rival leagues, such as the ABA, WFL and USFL offered higher salaries to sign players who would attract fans. But other than the old AFL, which ultimately merged with the NFL, no league presented a long-term threat to the NBA, NFL, MLB or NHL. (The American Basketball Assn. folded in 1976, but four of its teams joined the NBA.)

Youths take to the courts

I want to thank Spencer Haywood…for leading the way. Without Spencer Haywood there would be no Bill Willoughby, Darryl Dawkins, Moses Malone or myself.
—Kevin Garnett, after being named 2003-04 NBA MVP

In addition to suppressing wages though the reserve clause, owners united to control the minimum age at which players could enter their leagues. That way, the NBA and NFL could take advantage of a free farm system—college sports—without fear of any team undercutting the system by drafting a player below the minimum age.

Spencer Haywood left the University of Detroit in 1969 after two seasons. At the time, the NBA had a strict policy against drafting or signing a player until he was four years out of high school. Haywood played one season for the Denver Rockets of the ABA, was named MVP, then was signed by the Seattle SuperSonics. The NBA sued Haywood and Sonics owner Sam Schulman to keep Haywood out of the league.

At his first NBA game, lawyers served Haywood with an injunction ordering him to leave the arena. The public-address announcer reportedly said, "Ladies and gentlemen, we have an illegal player on the floor." Haywood endured racial slurs from fans. Even other NBA players turned their backs on him, thinking that by entering the league too young he had not played by the rules.

The case went all the way to the U.S. Supreme Court, which ruled that because Haywood was the only wage earner capable of taking care of his family, and therefore a "hardship case," he should be permitted to earn a living in the NBA.

Haywood's case paved the way for young players to declare themselves eligible for the NBA Draft, even right out of high school.

YOU BET YOUR LIFE

19

PLAYERS ASSOCIATIONS AND THE GOLDEN AGE

I'm tired of hearing about money, money, money.
I just want to play the game, drink Pepsi, wear Reebok.
—Shaquille O'Neal, product pitchman, NBA All-Star

Do you know...

?

- What a collective bargaining agreement (CBA) is? When your league's CBA expires? What the key issues are for the next CBA?
- What retirement benefits your league offers and how much of your contribution to the retirement fund your league matches?
- What type of health insurance benefits you are entitled to as a current player? As a former player?
- How you qualify for free agency?
- What the difference is between a strike and a lockout?
- How you file a grievance?

When it comes to representing professional athletes, most people think of sports agents. They rarely hear from a players association leader unless there is a strike or lockout. Players associations, however, constantly work behind the scenes to increase compensation and improve working conditions for their members.

While the commissioner of your league is hired by and works for the team owners, your players association is paid by you, through dues deducted from your paycheck, and works for you. The PA negotiates the CBA that determines your pay structure, benefits and working conditions. Your PA also certifies and oversees sports agents (to help protect you from incompetents, fraudsters and rip-off artists), files grievances for players, and collects data on salaries and shares it with agents to help them in their negotiations on behalf of players. In a nutshell, the PA's mission is to negotiate good CBAs and ensure that your rights under the CBA are protected. There's a lot of complex legal language in a CBA. As one players association official explained to PA members, "We have your back."

The PA works to protect your current interests and long-term financial security. The concept is simple: Working collectively, players have the leverage to negotiate better, fairer deals than if each player negotiated individually. In fact, there are many working conditions that would be difficult or impossible to negotiate individually. Here are just a few:

- The number and length of practices
- Number of exhibition games
- Length of playoff series
- Travel arrangements and road accommodations
- Policies and procedures regarding injuries
- Health benefits
- Pension plans

Before there were PAs, team owners unilaterally decided these issues, and there was little or nothing individual players could do about it.

Rookie orientation: Window into your new world

Your league has a rookie orientation program. Leagues have instituted hefty fines for rookies who don't show up. These programs are great opportunities to learn vital information.

Among the most useful parts of the rookie orientation are stories from league veterans about what they've done wrong: lost fortunes through bad investments or out-of-control spending or lost careers to drugs.

The programs coach rookies on how to cope with a world that most *twentysomethings* can hardly imagine. Role-playing exercises help you learn how to deal with (un)real world situations: media questions, requests for money, wily women, controlling the damage if you do slip up (everyone makes some kind of mistake). One of the most important aspects of rookie orientation is an introduction to your players association. Your professional career will be enriched if you show up day one thinking about how you can benefit from and contribute to your league and to your players association.

The collective bargaining agreement

Your CBA addresses the terms and conditions of employment, including wages, salary cap, heath benefits, retirement benefits, free agency, drug testing, agent certification, group licensing rights and grievance procedures. From the players' perspective the goal is simple: Get the best deal possible for all players. Each CBA establishes the players association as the exclusive collective bargaining agent for players.

Uniform Player Contract

Each league's CBA contains a uniform player contract (UPC) or a standard player contract. Your contract with your team is based on the UPC. The language is the same—"uniform" or "standard"—for every player, with blanks to be filled in regarding salary, signing bonus, length of contract and other variables. The UPC spells out the rights and remedies of both parties, and references the CBA throughout for further clarification.

It is not in the best interests of players to sign a contract drafted by ownership, nor one drafted by an individual agent, even one well versed in labor law. Players associations learn about many contingencies through the experience of all players, and they bargain to include them in the UPC. You do not have to reinvent the wheel.

When agents and PAs work together, you win

PAs have collectively bargained team salary caps and even salary minimums and maximums for different stages of a player's career. Some sports agents believe that by doing so the PAs have usurped their function. Other agents have accepted or even embraced the PAs and focused on the best possible representation of their players in the areas where agents can have an impact. For example, no players association can assess every team in the league and advise a free agent on where he has the best chance for a long and prosperous career.

The market for professional athletes moves fast and furious, like the stock market. A signing by one team often creates a ripple that affects several other players. If your agent works well with your PA and knows how to utilize its resources, you win. Your PA has every player contract in the league on file, and is eager to share that information with players and agents. How's that for data that can provide you and your agent with a comprehensive, detailed and up-to-the-minute understanding of the market? Furthermore, your PA has experts on contract language who, if consulted, can help your agent maximize benefits to you and avoid provisions that can come back to bite you.

Players associations have earned many victories, both big and small, but one of the most underrated advances on the labor front resulted from a legal case in which the union representing players in the North American Soccer League won access to player salary information. The lawyer who represented the union, Dick Berthelsen, later became the NFLPA general counsel.

According to the 1982 NFL Base Salary Directory, there were backup players earning more than starters. Minnesota Vikings starting quarterback Tommy Kramer, who threw for 3,912 yards in 1981, was earning $100,000, while 49er backup Guy Benjamin, who threw for 171 yards all season, was earning $130,000. Once players associations armed agents with salary information, players were no longer at such an informational disadvantage.

Said Berthelsen, "[Making salaries known to players and their representatives] made a very significant difference. Even more than we anticipated. What it did was make sure that false information was no longer being passed around."

The Golden Age

The Dark Ages have ended. You are fortunate to be playing in what, from the athlete's point of view, has to be the Golden Age of professional sports. The *minimum* salary in the NFL, NBA and MLB is well above the $203,000 per year earned by the Chief Justice of the U.S. Supreme Court. And he's a lot older than you, and had to pay to go to law school. In 2007, the *average* salary in the NFL is $1.8 million; in MLB, $3 million; in the NBA, $5.3 million.

Free agency has enabled players to command these big paychecks. Free agency, however, is not totally "free." Through CBAs negotiated by their PAs, athletes have recognized that owners have made an investment in young players, through signing bonuses, salaries and training/coaching. They have agreed that teams have the right to protect this investment for a few years before players are allowed to negotiate with other teams.

There are other limitations, such as in the NBA and NFL, "restricted free agents," and in the NFL, "exclusive franchise players," "non-exclusive franchise players" and "transition players." For more details, consult your PA Web site, PA office or your agent.

Why athletes are highly compensated

There are three reasons why pro athletes deserve every dollar they are paid:

1. Supply and demand. Professional athletes are the chosen few who, through a combination of good genes and hard work, possess the ability to play sports at the highest level. Out of every 1,000 kids who are good enough to compete in high school, perhaps one is able to make it into the pro ranks. Many want the job of pro athlete; few can perform it. Supply is tight. Demand, however, is enormous and growing. More and more people, in the United States and around the world, are shelling out more and more money to watch pro sports, in person and on television, including sponsors and direct payment by viewers.

2. Short careers. Depending on the sport, professional athletes play, on the average, for three to five years. Some can move into careers in coaching, sports management, broadcasting, or sports agency. For most pro athletes, however, the return on the years they (and their families) spent perfecting their skills must come during their relatively short time as pro athletes.

3. Risk. Injuries are an inherent part of pushing the limits of human performance, as professional athletes do every day. Unfortunately, many pro athletes end up with injuries that cause pain and limitation of activity for the rest of their lives. In capitalism, we compensate for risk. The saying goes: "No risk, no reward." Think of the converse: In exchange for great risk, athletes deserve to be highly compensated.

Those are the three reasons why pro athletes *deserve* their paychecks. The three reasons why they actually *receive* so large a share of team revenue, however, are the following:

1. The players associations
2. The movement of athletes that led to the players associations
3. The hard-earned right for free agency

Now that the players associations have won basic rights and a significant portion of league revenue for their players, they have evolved into being partners with, as well as adversaries of, the league owners. After all, it is in the interest of owners and athletes for the leagues to flourish. Every dollar that comes into the league is another dollar to be divided between players and owners. Be a good ambassador for your sport. "From the NBA perspective, they've got a product to sell," says Charles Barkley. "They've got to make it as attractive as possible to fans, viewers and corporate sponsors. Dr. J [Julius Erving] told me that we, the players, are the caretakers of the game."

Getting involved

As a professional athlete, it is in your best interest to become a knowledgeable member of your players association. Why?

➤ Salaries and benefits won by unified struggle can be lost by disinterest, passivity and looking out only for yourself.

➤ Players associations negotiate pension plans and benefits for their members. You will spend much more time as a former player than as an active player. But it is only as an active player that you get to influence and vote on terms that will be important to you and your family for decades to come.

➤ Through your players association, you can make contacts and accumulate knowledge and business skills that will help you for the rest of your life.

➤ Former players fought for you. The right thing to do is return the favor by fighting for their rights as retirees and by fighting for the rights of future players.

One way to become involved in your players association: Talk to your team's "player rep" and find out what's going on and, if you'd like to be an active member, how you can help. Make it a priority to attend as many association meetings as you can.

The wisdom of Marvin Miller

Marvin Miller was executive director of the MLBPA from 1966 to 1982. In 1968, he negotiated MLBPA's first collective bargaining agreement. In 1970, he negotiated for independent arbitration (previously the commissioner had sole authority to resolve all disputes). Miller was instrumental in Curt Flood's historic legal fight to overturn the reserve clause, which ultimately led to free agency. Hank Aaron called Miller "as important to the history of baseball as Jackie Robinson."

Today's professional athletes no longer fight with owners over fundamental rights. But players should not let their guard down.

In his 1991 book *A Whole Different Ball Game*, Miller articulated the role of the players association and the importance of continual player involvement. Wrote Miller: "I made sure that the players understood what I was doing, that they had input into decisions, that their reactions and ideas were seriously considered, that the information they needed to make intelligent decisions was theirs…I made sure that they understood the struggle involved in getting what they had…The minute we relaxed, we were greasing the skids for failure…If one side becomes too complacent, the other side becomes bolder."

Play or picket?

While there are still issues between players and owners, in 2007 the four major professional sports leagues enjoy labor peace. Thanks to favorable economic forces and past labor actions by PAs, today's professional athletes enjoy free agency and unprecedented salaries and benefits. Owners (except those in MLB) have salary caps. Team revenues and the values of teams are at all-time highs. Players and owners recognize how much they have to lose if either side initiates a work stoppage.

While it is far more pleasant to figure out how to divide billions of dollars than to fight over fundamental rights such as free agency, working conditions, and health and retirement benefits, there are no guarantees that labor peace will continue to prevail.

The membership of players associations are bound together by a common cause, but that doesn't mean everyone will agree 100% of the time. If you have disagreements, it's important to express yourself through the democratic union process. A strike is the absolute last option in labor negotiations, as is a lockout of players by owners. In the short run everyone loses, but some issues are worth fighting over. If your union's membership votes to strike, it is important to do everything in your power to support this decision by your actions and your words.

Another reason to save

I've stressed the benefits of saving money many times in this book. Here's yet another reason to save: No one ever wants to go on strike or be locked out, but withholding work is the ultimate negotiating tactic, the one that gives athletes the greatest leverage. If owners don't believe players have the resources to strike for a prolonged period, the threat of a strike doesn't scare them, and they are more likely to resort to a lockout to win concessions.

Final word

Most of this book is about what you can do on your own to help yourself. By working together with other players through your association, you can further guarantee your financial success. I encourage you to become an active participant in your players association.

THE HISTORY OF OWNER-PLAYER RELATIONS
THEN: WE OWN YOU!

NOW: WE LOVE THIS PARTNERSHIP!

PARTNERSHIP AND RIVALRY WITH OWNERS

They don't pay you a million dollars for two-hand chest passes.
—Pete Maravich, basketball star who in 1970 signed
the then-largest rookie contract ever ($1.6 million)

Baseball is too much a sport to be called a business,
and too much a business to be called a sport.
—P.K. Wrigley, longtime Chicago Cubs owner and chewing gum magnate

Chapter highlights

- There are still labor/management issues, but both sides recognize the importance of working together to maximize revenue.
- Do your part to promote the game: play with passion, be enthusiastic and give fans reasons to buy tickets and merchandise.

Owners of professional teams are a diverse group of individuals, from members of the Forbes 400 list of wealthiest Americans to those whose primary wealth has been derived from owning a professional team. Owners are mostly united in the goal to maximize league-wide revenue, but they definitely have different views on team revenue and team spending. Think about an owner who purchased a big-market team for $20 million in 1980, and an owner who purchased a similar team in 2004 for $1 billion, perhaps with the help of borrowed money that must be repaid with interest. There might be a big difference in their attitudes about how much return on investment they need to generate. They may also differ in their approach to their communities. Professional sports is a private business, but it also has quasi-public elements since teams receive some public funding and/or tax breaks to build stadiums, and all can be sources of civic pride.

Look through an owner's eyes

A good way to understand the owner(s) of your team and of other teams in your league is to put yourself in their shoes. If you owned a professional team, you would likely want to treat your players well, but you would also have a responsibility to earn a profit, especially if you had raised capital from other investors.

Seeing the league through management's eyes may have the added benefit of helping to prepare you for your post-playing career. Many athletes join management as announcers, coaches, assistant coaches, scouts, GMs, PR representatives, and in other executive capacities. A few have even become owners.

As an owner today, sure, you want to maximize revenue, but you realize that things aren't what they used to be (although perhaps you'd like them to be). The reserve clause is history; free agency, salary caps and revenue sharing are here to stay. Players associations give players the leverage to command high salaries.

Although your team may claim to lose money year after year, you are buoyed by the rising value of your franchise. And other businesses you own, such as regional sports networks and real estate in the area of your stadium, may justify operating your team at a loss. The profits from these ancillary businesses don't show up on the team's books, but they wouldn't exist without the team. Of course, you want to avoid or at least limit any losses on the team itself. Owning a professional sports franchise is a business, not a charity.

The management revolution

With the huge investment you've made in your players, you'd be smart to treat them well and earn their enthusiastic cooperation with your marketing efforts. You want to demonstrate to your players that you care about them as human beings, not just as commodities. Everything about your operation is first-class, from flying chartered jets to staying in five-star hotels.

Many teams even provide luxury locker rooms for opposing teams. Now that dirt-cheap wages and terrible benefits are no longer an option, raising your top line—revenue—is the key to raising your profits. You must compete for viewers and revenue with every other sport and every other form of entertainment.

The key to winning this competition is attracting fans. To attract fans, you, as a team owner, depend on your players to play five roles:

1. Athlete. Winning teams attract fans and can demand high ticket prices and other forms of revenue. Fans want to be astounded by an incredibly high level of performance. So of course you want your players to work hard to make the most of their athletic ability.

2. Entertainment. People are still talking about the home run Babe Ruth hit against the Chicago Cubs at Wrigley Field during the 1932 World Series. (Ruth reportedly stepped out of the batter's box and called his home run by pointing toward center field. A made-for-ESPN moment before the network even existed.) The public demands entertainment; as an owner, you want your athletes to find ways, in keeping with their individual personalities, to provide it. You do not want them saying, "I'm paid to play and that's it." For one thing, it's not true.

3. Community relations representative. You want people in your market area and, if possible, throughout the country or even the world to love the team you own. That means they have to identify with, like and respect many of the players. You want your players to sign autographs as if they enjoy it, to act in such a way that fans notice what nice, regular guys they are despite their amazing skills and all the money they make. You want your players to positively impact your community. You want them to visit schools, hospitals and other places where their presence can provide hope and inspiration.

4. Media relations representative. Most fans know players through the media. You want your athletes to be friendly and to cooperate with reporters.

5. Responsible adult. You have a big investment in your players. You do not want your phone to ring with news that a team member has been injured while bungee jumping, snowboarding or riding motorcycles, or been arrested for DUI, drugs or spousal abuse, or has thrown someone through a bar window. You want to hear stories about your players as dedicated family men who reach out to help those less fortunate.

Office of the commissioner

Each team owner faces a paradox. In the short run, an owner can maximize profit and/or competitive success by pursuing only the interests of his or her own team. But if every team owner does the same, the league would not flourish, and the individual teams would decline along with their league. One reason for this is the discrepancy in revenue between big-market and small-market teams. Clearly, TV networks pay more for the rights to Knicks or Lakers games than for, say, the Timberwolves' rights, because New York and Los Angeles have far more eyeballs to sell to sponsors than does Minneapolis.

To resolve this paradox, owners have empowered the commissioner to act in the best interests of the entire league, or, as they like to call it, "in the best interests of the game." Commissioners are charged with the responsibility of maintaining competitive balance. Revenue sharing and salary caps are the two primary mechanisms that leagues use to give all teams, regardless of the owner's wealth or the team's market size, a legitimate chance to compete.

Ever wonder why television and radio announcers regularly remind their audiences that "copying, rebroadcast or retransmission of this program without the express written consent of the office of commissioner is strictly prohibited"?

The owners and their representative, the commissioner, recognize that the flagship product sold by professional sports franchises is the right to broadcast games via television, radio and now other new media. Pro leagues and their teams grant media companies exclusive rights, in some form, through carefully crafted contracts. Local radio and television broadcasts bring in millions of dollars to individual teams. National television deals bring in billions, split evenly among every team. In order to protect the value of these deals, professional sports must do everything it can to minimize illegal uses of its property, including images, video and trademarks. The commissioner's office has been empowered to protect its copyright and go after infringers.

Commissioners serve many other critical league functions. The work of the commish is part ceremonial (shaking hands with David Stern on draft day is every aspiring basketball player's dream come true), part czar (the commissioner has broad powers to do what is necessary to carry out mandates to build league value), part ambassador (sports provides civic, even national, pride), and part management guru (getting 30 or so very different owners to agree takes masterful people skills).

In the past, perhaps commissioners played an adversarial role with players, but today the operative word is partnership. The success of each league is dependent on cooperation between owners and players, so commissioners work to cultivate positive relationships between owners and players.

NASCAR Nation

We live in a sports-crazed country. Check that—we live on a sports-crazed planet. On the world stage, soccer is arguably the most popular sport. But that's not the case in the United States. We're all about football, basketball, baseball and stock car racing.

Stock car racing? Yes. NASCAR has branched out throughout the country from its Southern roots. Its TV ratings are a consistent second only to the NFL. For reasons not entirely clear to many, NASCAR has captured the hearts—and wallets—of fans everywhere. NASCAR has sold the public on the total fan experience. It's not just watching the cars race around ovals. Famed "meet and greets" with NASCAR drivers provide fans with the opportunity to put a face and a personality to the men in the drivers' seats. Then fans can demonstrate their devotion by buying team merchandise.

Sponsors have taken note. Recognizing just how loyal the NASCAR fan base is, corporate America shells out tens of millions of dollars to associate with top NASCAR racing teams. The fans drive the NASCAR financial engine. They buy tickets, watch the races on TV and buy team products and the products of team sponsors (whose logos are constantly in view as cameras pan in on cars going 200 mph).

Other leagues are paying close attention. To compete for the public's entertainment dollar, leagues are implementing fan-friendly strategies modeled after NASCAR.

Go back to being an athlete

Now take off the owner's shoes and look at things again from your perspective as an athlete. The success of the leagues hinges on the relationship between management and players. Say owners may want to do something they believe will improve their businesses. In many cases, the CBA will require that they gain the approval of the players before instituting such change. Expanded playoff formats are recent examples. CBA provisions on revenue sharing require that there must be a mechanism to properly reward players with part of the income generated by additional playoff games.

Truth in accounting

It's a good thing for the players that their associations have secured a share of revenue rather than a share of profit. Many owners consistently maintain that they are losing money, despite annual increases in revenue (accompanied by larger payouts to players). Regardless of the owners' claims, data from the sale of teams shows that franchise values continue to trend upwards. If buyers believed the owners' figures, it would make no sense for them to risk ever-higher sums of money on pro teams whose balance sheets are consistently in the red.

Owners' cries of poverty may be negotiation posturing. Like good poker players, owners don't want their opponents to know the hand they're playing. Still, if they bluff every time they lose credibility, and their gains from this strategy diminish. Disagreements over the profitability of franchises and the reliability of team financial reports have strained relations between management and players over the years, and have even contributed to strikes and lockouts that have hurt both sides.

Eternal vigilance is the price of liberty

In an effort to maintain competitive balance, and therefore attract more fans and generate more revenue, the NFL, NBA and NHL have adopted salary caps. (In the NBA, wealthy owners can exceed the salary cap, but they must pay a "luxury tax" to the other owners.) In return for agreeing to team salary caps, players are guaranteed to receive a percentage of gross defined revenue. A few owners have been caught, in violation of the CBA, trying to shield, disguise or otherwise hide revenue. Cases are rare, but troubling. To prevent this, players associations audit the books. Even the best auditors can be fooled by outright deceit, but owners know that there could be serious legal and financial consequences if they are caught violating the CBA.

MLB has no salary cap yet and likely never will, but competitive balance is aided through revenue sharing. In 2006, the New York Yankees generated revenue of $302 million, while the Florida Marlins generated just $122 million. The redistribution of more than $300 million per year in TV and ticket revenue enables small-market teams to compete against wealthy franchises such as the Yankees, Red Sox, and Mets.

Changing attitudes toward undesirable behavior

Historically, punishment of illegal off-the-field behavior was left to the judicial system. That has changed.

On November 19, 2004, players from the NBA's Detroit Pistons and Indiana Pacers brawled on the court and in the stands. Some fans got into the action as well. Bill Walton, who was broadcasting the game for ESPN, said, "This is a low moment in NBA history...certainly no winners in this circumstance at all."

NBA Commissioner David Stern suspended Ron Artest of the Pacers for 86 games (73 regular season games plus 13 in the postseason) for his role in the incident. It was the longest suspension in NBA history for an infraction not related to drugs or gambling. Eight other players were suspended for a total of 60 games. (Five Pacers also faced criminal charges.)

In the 2007 off-season, NFL Commissioner Roger Goodell took unprecedented action against Cincinnati Bengals wide receiver Chris Henry and Tennessee Titans cornerback Adam "Pacman" Jones. Jones had committed a long series of offenses, culminating in assaulting a stripper in Las Vegas after "making it rain" dollar bills. Henry had multiple traffic violations and a DUI, then went to jail after he pleaded guilty to allowing minors to drink alcohol in his hotel room. Henry was suspended for eight games; Jones was suspended for the entire 2007 season. Jones' suspension may be shortened if he meets conditions set by the NFL.

Goodell had the express blessing of the NFLPA and of many players. Typically, players associations cry foul anytime a league flexes its muscles. But the vast majority of players conduct themselves in a socially appropriate manner and are becoming fed up with peers who repeatedly break the law, harming the image of their fellow athletes as they do so.

Players associations can file grievances on behalf of players accused of violating the rules, but historically, players lose most of these appeals. The commissioner's office has broad power to mete out punishment. Players who sign contracts with sponsors must also agree not to engage in acts of "moral turpitude."

Character = revenue

As owners compete for dollars against every other form of entertainment, they recognize that image impacts revenue. The NFL and other leagues want to polish and protect their images. The public wants its sports heroes appearing in United Way commercials.

Many league officials, commentators, even players, believe that in today's sports marketplace (with everything seemingly exposed in the media), "bad behavior" translates into lost revenue.

Players associations must and do protect athletes by demanding due process (e.g., by filing grievances that are heard by independent arbitrators). Most sports law scholars agree, however, that league commissioners have broad power in these matters, particularly when PAs are in agreement. In April 2007, the NFL inaugurated sanctions for conduct that undermines or puts at risk the integrity and reputation of the league. The policy includes:

- larger fines and longer suspensions
- harsher treatment of repeat violations, even without a legal conviction
- expansion of the annual rookie symposium to include mandatory year-round rookie orientation by all clubs
- a mandatory, expanded annual life-skills program for all players and clubs
- annual mandatory briefings by local law enforcement reps for all players and clubs

Conclusion: From owners to commissioners to players, the trend in professional sports is to come down hard on the so-called "bad apples." Playing professional sports is a privilege, not a right. Teams and leagues have broad powers to fine, suspend, even permanently banish players whose behavior is illegal.

Part Seven

BEYOND THE FIELD

How to Relate to the Media and Fans

Learn your clichés. Study them. Know them.
They're your friends. Write this down:
"We gotta play one game at a time."
"I'm just happy to be here and hope I can help the ballclub."
—Crash Davis to Nuke LaLoosh in the movie, "Bull Durham"

I didn't say I didn't say it. I said that I didn't say that I said it.
I want to make that very clear.
—George Romney, Michigan governor and presidential candidate

In previous chapters we discussed the importance of selling the game and how that encompasses far more than simply just showing up and playing hard. The media plays a vital role in shaping public perception, both good and bad. Connie Mack, who made his professional baseball debut in 1882 and then managed the old Philadelphia A's for 50 years, understood the role of the media. He said, "When I entered the game, [sports] received only a few lines as news. These few lines extended into columns and pages. In ratio the crowds in our ball parks grew and grew and grew. News, like advertising, is a powerful momentum behind any enterprise. The professional sporting world was created and is being kept alive by the services extended by the press."

Journalists make a living with words, so I asked some of them (and some present and former pro athletes) to comment on how athletes should relate to the media. After that, we'll talk about the "role model" question in this Internet/video-camera-in-a-cellphone era of total and instant visibility.

A number of sports reporters have said that one of the worst things an athlete can do is to always have an agent or PR person speaking for him. Fans—who ultimately pay athletes' salaries—want to hear directly from athletes themselves.

Remarks by sports journalists and athletes

T.J. Simers
Los Angeles Times
"You might want to learn from the very start how to avoid getting tagged with a stupid nickname. That's why I begin with the Boston Parking Lot Attendant, the guy who bought the Los Angeles Dodgers, telling the media at his first press conference that 'the Dodgers baseball fans are the greatest in all of baseball.' OK, so I asked, what would you have told the fans in Boston had you been successful in your attempt to buy the Red Sox? B.S. kills. It numbs, it does not flatter, and it does not do you any favors. Maybe the media goes away, but then so goes your notoriety, your chance to cultivate an ally, and your opportunity to make a connection with the public—which comes in handy when times get tough. One simple fact: There is no such thing as an objective reporter. Reporters shade the truth to make someone really look good when they like someone, someone who has taken an interest in them and maybe asked about their family or interests in life. Reporters shade the truth to make someone look like a horse's ass when they don't like someone, and God help you if you provide the ammunition for them to bring out the cannons. By the way, the Boston Parking Lot Attendant's name is Frank McCourt. He might've gotten off to a better start—rather than emphasizing his experience as a parking lot owner before buying the Dodgers—if only he had been more straightforward. But then again, it is a good nickname."

Robert Lipsyte
New York Times
"In the mid-1990s, after a career avoiding hockey because I didn't get it, I spent a season writing frequent columns about the New York Rangers for the New York Times because Adam Graves took the time after practice—probably less than a half hour—to explain the tactics of a wing protecting his star center. It opened a window for me and led to more informed questions and hopefully more intelligent columns. The players let me know they appreciated their hard work being explained. Graves treated me like a professional—ultimately all most reporters want—and in return I was able to treat him like one instead of some object of resentment or false adoration."

Art Spander
Oakland Tribune, Pro Football Hall of Fame inductee
"When it comes to athletes dealing with the media, understand that as you do your job, the media needs to do its job, which is reporting and commenting on sports. That leads to communication and cooperation. The more the better. Also, within limits, honesty. Better not to say anything than to lie or mislead.

Everyone wants good press, naturally. But there are times when the reporting is critical because it has to be. Will Clark, the former San Francisco Giants first baseman, told me once, 'My college coach told me to be positive, and you're always negative.' My response was that we have different obligations. If you're 0 for 40, you're only supposed to think about getting a hit the next at-bat. I, on the other hand, am supposed to write that you're 0 for 40 and ask you why."

Fred Claire
Former Los Angeles Dodgers general manager
"One time there was something written about our team which I thought was completely unfair. My first reaction was to respond immediately in order to set the record straight. But Walter [O'Malley, then owner of the Dodgers] stopped me. He did not want me to get involved in things which ultimately had no bearing on our team and its performance. His line, which I've repeated often, was, 'Don't argue with people who buy ink by the barrel.' Stay focused on your objectives. Ultimately, you'll be judged by your accomplishments or lack of accomplishments, but don't let the media determine your fate."

Alexander Wolff
Sports Illustrated
"If I had to advise athletes on how to treat the press and the fans, I would probably describe a very poignant scene: Listening to the greatest scorer in NBA history, a former Sports Illustrated Sportsman of the Year, sitting in a small office in a high school on an Indian reservation in Arizona, ruing that his standoffish posture for so many years had essentially foreclosed his ability to hook on as a coach in the league he once dominated. One of the most memorable moments of my career, listening to Kareem Abdul-Jabbar that day."

Len Elmore
Former NBA player, lawyer, broadcaster, president, NBRPA
"Athletes must remember that this is a game and it is, in the final analysis, entertainment. It's not war. It's not life or death. Keep everything in perspective. Learn to communicate clearly and unambiguously where possible. The fans are your constituents. In many ways fans are responsible for how much you are paid. Keep that in mind when you're dealing with fans and media (who speak to your constituents on a regular basis). Treat fans and media with respect and professionalism until and unless they forfeit that right by their conduct toward you. In a situation where you feel mistreated, keep your cool and try not to escalate the situation any further."

Shelley Smith
ESPN

"We in the media love to roll our eyes and yawn when we hear an athlete deliver clichés. But when one is bold enough to say something closer to the truth, we love to criticize him or her for that as well. My advice: Avoid clichés at all costs. Give us anecdotal evidence as to why you believe something to be true and above all, be prepared to defend your position if it is controversial. Keyshawn Johnson and I wrote a book after his miserable 1-15 season with the New York Jets in 1996. It was controversial. It was outlandish. But he stood by what he believed and didn't back off, even when faced with incredible heat from the New York media. I'll always respect him for that."

Rick Telander
Chicago Sun-Times

"The media-athlete relationship is a complex and often sticky one, but at its root, it's a simple one. It's about two people talking. Truth, courtesy, respect. The stupid questions that will invariably come from media reps can be answered without anger or disgust by athletes, as curtly as needed. The bad timing of tough questions—after a hard loss, during a difficult personal time—is truly, maybe even sadly, part of the game. So it goes."

Labor relations and the media

During the 1999 NBA lockout, a player joked to a reporter, "I may have to sell a couple of my cars to make ends meet." The player, who devoted some of his multimillion-dollar salary to collecting exotic cars, may have thought nothing of tossing off the quip. When it hit the media, however, the joke was on him, his fellow players and the players association. TV sports commentators and print journalists jumped on this opportunity to talk about today's "spoiled, filthy rich athletes" who are so "out of touch" with ordinary people who can hardly afford to attend their games. Team owners were delighted about this diversion from the real issues that pro athletes face, such as short careers, injuries and the right to a significant portion of the revenue generated by their talent, skill and dedication to conditioning. In talking to the media, a little bit of humbleness can go a long way toward relating to the average fan, who may have a hard time understanding why salaries in the millions, or even hundreds of thousands per year, are not enough for today's athletes.

During periods of contract negotiations, players should be especially careful to think before they talk to the media, and to either not comment or make only statements supportive of their players association and its demands. Generally, it's best to leave the comments about labor disputes to those designated by the players association to speak on its behalf.

Are you a role model?

Charles Barkley once famously declared, "I am not a role model." Fellow NBA great Karl Malone, however, said, "We don't choose to be role models; we are chosen."

Ironically, Barkley's comment was part of a Nike ad campaign. Nike obviously thought that youngsters would follow Sir Charles' example, at least in their shoe-buying behavior.

"I don't believe professional athletes should be role models," Barkley explained. "I believe parents should be role models…It's not like it was when I was growing up. My mom and my grandmother told me how it was going to be. If I didn't like it, they said, 'Don't let the door hit you in the ass on your way out.'"

No doubt that parents' behavior has a profound impact on their kids. But a Kaiser Family Foundation survey (October 2000) supports Malone's argument: 73% of children ages 10 to 17 selected athletes as their role models. That probably means that at least 73% of parents want athletes to behave in a way that will influence their kids in a good direction. These parents and their kids are ticket-buying, merchandise-buying, TV-watching fans. That means 100% of owners and league commissioners want their players to behave admirably.

Top Ten Tips for Dealing with the Media

Be personal
Make eye contact. Call reporters by their first name. Be friendly even when they're not interviewing you.

Be prepared
Think about what you want to say beforehand. For postgame interviews, take a minute to collect your thoughts. For feature stories, outline key points in your mind or on paper.

Be professional and respectful
Show up on time for scheduled interviews. Understand the writer's job is to report good and bad. Don't take anything personally.

Be engaging
Give thoughtful, not stock, answers. Appropriate humor is welcome. Good-natured trash-talking is fine if that's you. No ethnic, gender or religious slurs or insults. Give concise answers.

Be accommodating
Befriend the media. They are your ally—or your worst enemy.

Don't go there
What happens in the locker room stays in the locker room. Don't air your dirty laundry in public. And avoid clichés!

Know how and when to "no comment"
It's OK to courteously not comment on something you're asked. As Plato once said, "Wise men speak because they have something to say; fools because they have to say something."

Do not lie or mislead
If you're asked a question you're not prepared to answer, speak the truth or not at all. The lie is often bigger than the original misdeed.

Avoid off the record
Don't hide behind anonymity. Embrace the new reality that there are no secrets. Eventually, everything comes out.

Act like this is fun
After all, it's still just a game!

TEDDY, YOU'RE AN ATHLETE'S BEST FRIEND.
YOU MAY BEG FOR TREATS, BUT YOU
NEVER ASK FOR MONEY.

INVOLVEMENT IN THE COMMUNITY

Too often we underestimate the power of a touch, a smile, a kind word,
a listening ear, an honest compliment, or the smallest act of caring,
all of which have the potential to turn a life around.
—Leo Buscaglia, professor and author

Chapter highlights

- Helping your community is good for your community and good for you.
- When it comes to charity, you will be pressed for your money and time.
- Be professional in every sense.

Thousands of national and local charitable organizations depend on the time, energy and money of volunteers to deliver services to the community. And new charitable organizations and foundations are founded on a daily basis. Our tax code supports charitable giving by enabling people to deduct a portion of their donations from their income taxes to qualified organizations.

I encourage you to get involved in the community. The reasons are simple and straightforward. One, you are among the most privileged members of society, blessed with good health and unbelievable fortune. Two, you have a chance to touch lives, especially young children, in so many unique ways. Three, your stature as a professional athlete can help mobilize others to join a cause you care about. Four, involvement in nonprofits is a networking opportunity.

Finally, "giving back" to the community is expected of you. "Teams see player philanthropy as critical," reported *The Wall Street Journal* (April 28, 2007), "in part because of a widening rift between athletes and fans. Players' salaries have hit astronomical levels, even as leagues have had to crack down on player misconduct." The article quotes Bernie Mullin, CEO of the NBA's Atlanta Hawks and NHL's Atlanta Thrashers, "Fans have to relate to the players as people...We sit down with every player to find out about their lives and families to see if there's a cause that's touched their lives...It's not 100% altruistic—we're a business."

Not all charities are created equal

After all I've said about the importance of applying due diligence to selecting professional advisers, it will probably not come as a shock to you that I recommend being equally careful about lending your support to a charity. Unfortunately, not every charitable organization lives up to its lofty goals. The primary financial measurement of a charity is efficiency: the percentage of money raised which goes directly to services that support the organization's mission. Giving at least 75% of funds raised to charitable programs is considered efficient. Small charitable foundations, unless they are run mainly by volunteers, can find this difficult because they do not enjoy the economies of scale of large charities.

Is community involvement starting to sound like work? There is probably some truth to the aphorism, "No good deed goes unpunished." There are even fraudsters who have discovered they can set up charities, collect funds from well-meaning people, and use the money for their own ends. Obviously, it's critical to avoid being associated with such morally bankrupt people and organizations. Several pro athletes have been burned by such involvement. But the main point is that when you donate your time, energy and money appropriately, you can make a significant impact by helping people who face serious problems.

Start slowly. Lend your name only to a charity you have gotten to know through a longstanding relationship. Leagues and teams are active in communities. "NBA Cares" is an example. The leagues carefully vet the charities they support. Team owners, too, are often pillars of the philanthropic communities in their cities. Through the league and your team, you can find legitimate charities without having to do a lot of your own research. This can be a big help, particularly at the beginning of your career and your charitable giving. Be careful as well about establishing your own charitable foundation. While you may have the best intentions, your name is on the line. Some pro athletes and other celebrities have started charities, hired friends and family to manage them ("Charity begins at home"?), and been burned by mismanagement or even theft. Charities are required to publicly disclose financial data. If your charity is not efficiently managed, you are likely to face criticism, even if your only motive was to do good.

Many foundations established by pro athletes have accomplished wonderful things. If you are going to create a charitable foundation, perhaps the best time to do it is when you are well established, have done well financially, and can attract top people for the board and hire top professionals to help run the foundation.

Bottom line: Give. Carefully.

Resources

Charity Navigator rates large charities on their efficiency. It works to "advance a more efficient and responsive philanthropic marketplace by evaluating the financial health of America's largest charities." Web site: charitynavigator.org.

Guide Star posts IRS Form 990 and other information on 1.5 million tax-exempt nonprofits. Form 990 details a charity's income, sources of income, and expenses. Guidestar's mission is to create a "more transparent and accountable nonprofit community…Accurate information is a powerful tool, and our users have responded with better-informed, more effective giving decisions." Web site: guidestar.org.

Professionalism in community relations

In relations with the community and the media, a little effort produces a big reward. Every interaction is an opportunity to sell yourself, your team and your league. Unfortunately, it's also an opportunity to bungle the sale. Athletes (and other celebrities) have a reputation for being unreliable when it comes to showing up for scheduled appearances. They may be no flakier than anyone else, but in the case of the average Joe, who's counting?

Here are some commonsense suggestions for creating and maintaining a solid reputation:

Know your schedule: Probably the best approach is to have and use a password-protected program such as Microsoft Outlook. If you don't keep your own schedule, make sure you have one person to coordinate it, otherwise there will definitely be double bookings. Review your schedule daily. Make sure logistics are worked out, including exact addresses and phone numbers for problems or emergencies.

Travel: If it's local, do you have directions? Are they going to send a driver? If you have to travel to another city, make sure everything—including plane ticket, hotel and transportation—is taken care of to your satisfaction. Don't be a diva. Make reasonable requests. Ask politely.

Prioritize: Schedule your training first. Then understand the pecking order. Make sure that you do what is asked of you by your team and your sponsors. During the off-season you have more flexibility to fit your training schedule around events.

Say no: Always be courteous. If it's a charitable organization, send back a short personal letter (preferably handwritten). Something to this effect: *I am honored to be invited to your event. I am very impressed by the work your organization does to [fill in what they do]. Unfortunately my schedule does not permit me to participate [or cite specific travel conflict]. Keep up the good work.* If you think it is a worthy cause that you want to support, send a donation or an autographed jersey to auction (if they are having an auction).

Keep your word: Many worthy causes may seek your services, including youth organizations, hospitals, military, mentally or physically challenged, on and on. You can do a few of them, but not all. If you do give your word that you will speak at or attend an event, honor your commitment. If a legitimate emergency prevents you from doing so, make it up to the charity by sending a check or rescheduling your appearance.

TRANSITION GAME

Athletes die twice.
—Jackie Robinson, Hall of Fame baseball player

Chapter highlights

- Now is the time to prepare for life as a former professional athlete.
- Financial security is important, but so is career fulfillment.
- Get educated about money.

For Chapter 21, I asked journalists to provide advice on relating to the media. This chapter features advice from current and former pro athletes on preparing for life after your career as a professional athlete is over.

When should you start preparing for that moment? Now. The consensus of the contributors to this chapter is that it's never too early to work on the skills that lead to successful retirement:

➤ Saving money
➤ Investing wisely
➤ Developing business/financial/people savvy
➤ Gaining knowledge and proficiency that can lead to a new career
➤ Developing healthy interests that can replace the intense focus on your sport

More than Magic; it's hard work

Most of the stories in this book are about athletes who made bad decisions. Away from the game, an athlete is noticed primarily when he or she messes up, just as an offensive lineman is noticed mainly when he misses a block or is called for a penalty. But many professional athletes have quietly gone on to lucrative and satisfying business careers. Earvin "Magic" Johnson is an outstanding example. As a 6-foot 9-inch point guard for Michigan State and for the Los Angeles Lakers, Magic Johnson revolutionized the game of basketball. He led Michigan State to the NCAA Championship in 1979, then led the Lakers to five NBA titles. Instead of making him play inside, coaches recognized his unique ability to be a big man who could handle the ball, read the court, and create plays. Magic has proven equally adept in the business world, as chairman and CEO of Magic Johnson Enterprises.

Here are excerpts from what Magic said at a conference I attended in August 2007:

- "I was a basketball player, but I was setting up for a successful business career. Everything I learned in basketball I can use in business."
- "Business is competitive. I hate to lose, but I learn from losing."
- "I had to take my ego out and say, Earvin, you don't know business. So I went out and found people who knew more than I did. I approached successful businessmen, many of who came to Lakers games. These guys liked sports, but they weren't making their living in the sports business."
- "I concluded it takes the same effort to become a great businessman as it does to be a great basketball player. Business is a fascinating world with its own language. Instead of fastbreaks and Showtime, it's interest rates and EBITDA."

A *Forbes* article in 1996 provided a particular example of how Magic built his connections to business people: "He befriended Joe Smith, the powerful president of Warner Bros. Records, now a music business consultant, who sat courtside for every Laker home game. Over dinner one night in Hollywood's Le Dome restaurant, Smith introduced Johnson to agent Michael Ovitz.

"Thus was born an informal Magic Johnson advisory group he labeled Team Magic. It included Ovitz, Smith, a local business attorney, John Argue, Lakers promotions chief Lon Rosen, and two business managers, Warren Grant and Joel Ehrenkranz. Recalls Smith: 'We told him to be careful who you trust, and never give anyone too much trust.'"

According to the Forbes article, "At a projected $5-million-plus in ticket sales for this year, [Johnson's] Baldwin Hills [Calif.] theater has become one of the top-grossing movie outlets in the country. Another one opened in urban

Atlanta last month. A dozen more are coming within the next three years. It's the start of what Johnson's advisers say is an all-out bid to become America's most important black entrepreneur.

"Starting modestly with a T-shirt licensing company, Johnson has built a $60-million-a-year business, including concert promotions, a traveling performance team, adult and children's basketball camps, 5% ownership of the Lakers plus a stake in planned or existing commercial real estate projects. Forbes figures Johnson's net worth is edging up to $100 million. And the best is yet to come.

"'It's important to help the community, but the number one goal here is to make money,' Johnson says. 'This is not charity.'"

Here's what other former professional athletes have to say:

Ralph Cindrich, sports agent, former NFL player

On life after pro sports:
"My advice to professional athletes, particularly those who play football: Get what you can out of the game and get out without a crippled body. War heroes and star athletes die a fast public death. Start now preparing for your life without athletics. Hire honest, competent professionals, not friends, and understand nothing comes easy that is worthwhile. Learn about business, taxes, investments and all that is taking place with your money. Watch and follow closely respected leaders and copy them. Associate yourself only with winners and positive people. Whatever it is you want to do with the greater portion of your life, start it now while you are hot because you may never be there again."

Steve Kerr, general manager, Phoenix Suns, five-time NBA champion

On developing interests beyond your sport:
"As a group, professional athletes are really focused. This makes sense, since we're paid to be good at our sport. Still, it's important to have something that interests you when you're done playing—a hobby, a new career, golf, whatever. Obviously, athletes need to save money while they're playing, but a lot of guys who are OK financially end up bored once they're done. That makes the transition to 'real life' more difficult."

On your sport:
"Professional athletes are risk-takers, but we're still terrified of failure. A bad practice, a bad game or sometimes even a bad shot can draw the ire of the coach, if not the fans. The best advice I ever received was from Michael

Jordan. He told me, 'Don't be afraid to miss.' MJ's point was to prepare like heck and then go out and play. If you have doubts, your fears will come true."

On business:
"Make sure you understand your own finances, rather than have someone else taking care of everything. It's easy to hire someone to do everything, but if you pay your own bills and balance your own checkbook, you're more likely to have control of your money. If you're removed from the process, you will have a tough time making sense of what's going on and will, by default, make decisions based on what others tell you."

On training:
"Remember that it's your job: Do it every day, even when you don't feel like it. Your physical conditioning is your livelihood. There are so few jobs in professional sports. Guys are hungry to get in the league—and hungry to stay in the league. If you are fortunate to have a job as a professional athlete, realize you can lose it in an instant, either by injury or by not improving."

Charles Barkley, TNT analyst, NBA Hall of Famer

On saving money:
"After you grow up and you're poor, I don't think there's anything like when you go to the NBA and you have all this money. It's a culture shock. Unless you are careful and strong, you can go broke in a hurry...I tell all these young kids, the money you make, save it, put it in the bank. That money has to last you the rest of your lifetime, don't waste it."

On economic reality:
"Too many professional athletes can't control their newfound wealth. To a lot of us, signing a multimillion-dollar contract is a like winning the lottery. We see what we think is the contract's bottom line—the dollar signs—but fail to see the true bottom line: economic reality after taxes."

On the language of money:
"For many of us, the life of wealth is like living in a foreign country. We're not prepared to deal with the differences, to understand anything anyone is telling us or to know the local customs. Sooner or later, if we're lucky, we eventually learn the language, but not before making a lot of costly mistakes and maybe even embarrassing ourselves numerous times."

On loaning friends money:
"I lent millions of dollars to people I'll never see again. If you don't, they say, 'You're not black anymore. You're too good for us.' When you're young, you take that stuff to heart...I used to have a problem telling the people I love, 'No, I can't.'"

Curtis Martin, former NFL star running back

On the pressure put on athletes by families:
The type of pressure that friends and family can put on you is unbelievable.
One thing that I always try to preach to some of the younger athletes is to get
good at saying no. Most of us feel so obligated because we are the only one,
probably in our entire generation of our family tree, who has had this kind of
success. The whole tree comes after you. When to say no and when to say yes,
on top of trying to have a successful career, is overwhelming many times...
One of the most difficult parts of being a professional athlete is dealing with
that whole tree coming after you, and dealing with the pressure of taking care
of not only your own family, but every family that's even close to you. If you
don't have anyone to help you sift through that process, it's extremely hard...I
think the general public equates wisdom with money, and there's nothing
further from the truth. People wonder, with all the money you make, how
could you do something that stupid? I think that more money opens you up
to doing something that stupid.

Danny Ainge, general manager, Boston Celtics, former NBA player

On agents and dependency:
"Professional athletes need to understand the business they are in. You don't
have to be an expert, but you need to know what's going on. Too many agents
want to keep their guys in the dark and dependent on their services. Agents
and financial advisers should help prepare players for life, teaching them
about business—how to pay bills, how to read and understand financial
statements, how to negotiate. You can't learn this stuff overnight, but you have
to be willing to put in time reading and listening."

10 Challenges of Retirement

By Ken Ruettgers, former NFL player

1. Denial: You've been trained your entire career to "be tough," to "never give up or give in," and to "play through the pain." You've maintained the image and illusion of "having it all together." Every athlete must face post-career transition, and denial only prolongs the process. Not only can living in denial derail you financially, but it can also derail your marriage—and more.

Truth: If you think you're not challenged by retirement, you haven't been out of the game long enough, or you're lying to yourself.

2. Divorce: Of all NFL marriages that fail, 50% fail in the first year after leaving the game. It takes extreme focus and sacrifice to be a professional athlete. To some degree you've probably neglected your marriage and other relationships.

Truth: When you retire from the game, relationships that took a backseat during your playing career must become a priority.

3. Financial loss and challenges: The average NFL player's salary is more than 25 times the average U.S. household income. You've enjoyed the good life. Some players have been generous to family and friends along the way (maybe too generous). But you've worked too hard and too long during your career to lose everything after retiring.

Truth: It's not how much you make, but how much you're able to keep that counts.

4. Physical challenges: 65% of NFL players retire with permanent injuries. You've put your body through hell and back—training, practice and playing. Now the game is over and it's difficult to admit that you may be physically disabled. Now your motivation is not as intense, and you may gain weight and generally find yourself out of shape.

Truth: You need to take care of your body like never before. You're not "10 feet tall and bullet-proof" anymore.

5. Lack of purpose: *Newsday* reported in 1997 that more than half of retired professional athletes believe they've lost their purpose in life. You were born to play sports—now what? Even if you had enough money to retire—and you might—you can't stare at the walls all day.

Truth: Whatever follows pro sports will feel like a step down.

6. Anger, bitterness and jealousy: Many athletes do not retire willingly. The game can leave you behind. You're injured, cut, too old or a victim of the salary cap. It's easy to point fingers. Whatever the reason, you're no longer playing professional sports.

Truth: If you don't meet this challenge head on, these natural emotions will prevent you from making a successful transition.

7. Loss of structure: Playing is a grind: training camp, working on Sundays and holidays. Maybe you hated it. Ah, retirement! The good life. No one telling you where to be and what to do. No direction. No foundation. No structure. It can also be unsettling.

Truth: Structure is a love/hate relationship that will take some time to balance during transition.

8. Isolation: The guys that are still playing are busy with their careers trying to win a world championship, to secure a spot on the team, and build their own personal wealth. If you could only find someone to talk to who understands, but only a player would know—a retired player. Isolation is a challenging part of post-career transition.

Truth: There are many resources available for retired professional athletes. You just have to reach out.

9. Substance abuse: Substance abuse can destroy any hope of a successful transition after football. Turning to drinking or illegal or prescription drugs only prolongs the agony of retirement and transition and leaves a wake of destruction behind. Leaving the game is painful, and you will try to find relief—one way or another.
Truth: The most difficult drug to put behind you is the NFL.

10. Depression: If the first nine challenges haven't depressed you already, this will: The suicide rate among former NFL players is nearly six times the national average. More than one in five Americans suffer from clinical depression.

Truth: If you're feeling depressed, you're not alone. Seeking treatment for depression can be a tough but critical step.

Ken Ruettgers played 12 years for the Green Bay Packers. He is the founder of GamesOver.org, a nonprofit group dedicated to helping former professional athletes cope with the stress of retirement.

Appendix A: League information

Note: This information about the leagues is as of September 2007.

National Football League

Headquarters	Union
National Football League 280 Park Ave New York, NY 10017 (212) 450-2000 NFL.com	NFLPA 2021 L Street, NW, Suite 600 Washington, DC 20036 (800) 372-2000, (202) 463-2200 NFLPA.com

Leader	**Commissioner** Roger Goodell	**NFLPA Executive Director** Gene Upshaw	
Roster Spots	45 (+8 on practice squad)	**Salaries as % of total revenues**	59.5% of designated revenue (amount varies because certain club revenue is not shared)

Minimum Salaries	
Rookie	$285,000
One Year	$360,000
Two Years	$435,000
Three Years	$510,000
Four to Six Years	$595,000
Seven to Nine Years	$720,000
Ten or More Years	$820,000

Free Agency Eligibility	
Unrestricted	4 years
Restricted	3 years
Exclusive Rights	Less than 3 years

Benefits	
Severance	Once a player retires or is released (with at least two "credited" seasons in the league), he receives a lump-sum of $10,000 for every credited year he played.
401(k)	The NFL matches each players' 401(k) investments 2-for-1, up to the first $10,000. (If you put in $10,000, the NFL puts in $20,000.) If a player elects not to contribute his own pre-tax savings, the NFL must still put $3,600 into player's 401(k) account. In 2006, the maximum individual contribution was $15,000.
Pension Plan	Referred to as Bert Bell/Pete Rozelle NFL Player Retirement Plan. Eligibility: 3 years on NFL roster (prior to 1992, 4 years required). Benefit: League pays $425 per month per season played. Players must be at least 55 to collect full benefits.

NFL, continued

Line of Duty Disability	If a player suffers a career-ending injury from football (but he is not totally and permanently disabled), he may be eligible for "Line of Duty" disability benefits. The benefit is the greater of $1,000 per month or 100% of a player's monthly pension amount. A player must apply for this benefit within 4 years of leaving NFL. The player can collect these payments for 7.5 years. This benefit is paid in addition to any workers' compensation benefits the player may receive.
Post-career Health Insurance	Full health insurance coverage is extended for 5 additional years for "vested" players (someone with at least 3 credited seasons). A credited season is a season spent on an NFL roster or injured reserve, but not on a practice squad, for at least 3 games.
Medical Savings Account	The NFL now offers a medical savings account. The account can be used to fund post-career medical insurance, including the COBRA premium, and to pay other medical expenses for the player and his dependents. Clubs contribute $25,000 a year, up to a total of $300,000, which can cover medical costs of a player and his family. For example, a 12-year veteran will leave the NFL with a $300,000 health reimbursement account. The account kicks in 5 years after retirement (when a player's NFL post-career medical insurance coverage runs out). The account does not earn interest.
Collective Bargaining Agreement runs through 2011	

National Basketball Assn.

Headquarters	Union
National Basketball Assn. 645 Fifth Avenue New York, NY 10022 (212) 407-8000 NBA.com	National Basketball Players Assn. 310 Lenox Avenue New York, NY 10027 (212) 655-0880 NBPA.com

Leader		**Commissioner** David Stern	**NBPA Executive Director** Billy Hunter	
Roster Spots		14 (12 active, up to 3 inactive)	**Salaries as % of total revenues**	57% of basketball related income
Minimum Salaries				
Rookie			$427,163	
One Year			$687,456	
Two Years			$770,610	
Three Years			$798,328	
Four Years			$826,046	
Five Years			$895,341	
Six Years			$964,636	
Seven Years			$1,033,930	

NBA, continued

Free Agency Eligibility
Free agent eligibility in the NBA is dependent upon: 1) If the player was drafted in the first round, in which case the player could be an unrestricted free agent after his second year if his team does not pick up the option to his contract, after his third year if his team does not pick up the option to his contract, or after his fourth year if his team does not tender him a qualifying offer. Should the team tender the qualifying offer, the player is a restricted free agent. 2) If the player was drafted in the second round, in which case the player's free agency eligibility will be determined by the contract he signs upon entering the league. 3) If the player was not drafted, in which case the player's free agency eligibility will be determined by the contract he signs upon entering the league.

Benefits	
401(k)	A player can contribute up to $15,000 (determined by law) to the plan and teams will match 140% of the contribution.
Player Supplemental Medical Benefit	This benefit is intended to provide certain health-related benefits to players who have played in the NBA since the 2000-2001 season.
Labor-Management Cooperation and Education Trust	This trust is designed to provide HIV/AIDS education programs and education and career counseling programs.
Pension Plan	A defined benefit retirement plan with a contractually established monthly benefit amount determined by years of service. Players who have played at least 3 seasons are eligible for benefits. League pays at least $385 per month per season played. Example: A player with six years' experience would receive $2,310 per month. Players can take a lump sum payment at age 50 or receive monthly benefits beginning at age 62. The plan includes cost of living adjustments.

Collective Bargaining Agreement runs through 2011, but league could extend it through 2012. CBA can be terminated early if: 1) collusion occurs (NBPA may terminate), 2) national broadcast revenue drops significantly (NBA may terminate), 3) it is economically impractical to run the league (NBA may terminate), 4) court proceedings determine CBA is unlawful (either side may terminate).

Major League Baseball

Headquarters		Union	
Major League Baseball 245 Park Avenue New York, NY 10167 (212) 931-7800 MLB.com		Major League Baseball Players Assn. 12 East 49th Street, 24th Floor New York, NY 10017 (212) 826-0808 MLBPlayers.com	
Leader	**Commissioner** Allan H. (Bud) Selig	**MLBPA Executive Director** Donald M. Fehr	
Roster Spots	24 minimum, 40 for playoffs	**Salaries as % of total revenues**	63% of baseball-related income

Minimum Salary
$380,000

Free Agency Eligibility
A player is eligible for free agency with 6 or more years of MLB service. A player becomes eligible for salary arbitration with 3 or more years of MLB service, but less than 6 years. It is possible to be eligible after 2 years of MLB service if the player has at least 86 days of service during the immediately preceding season and ranks in the top 17% of players who have 2 years but less than 3 years of MLB service.

Benefits	
Pension Plan	Each member of the players' union will receive a benefit at the time of retirement, with the amount being equal to the player's accrued benefit, which is the sum of the player's fixed retirement benefit and assumed variable benefit.
Investment Plan	Contributions are made to member accounts for players who have at least 60 days of active service and have accrued at least one quarter of a year of active service. Contributions are determined by a specific amount per quarter year of service.
Welfare Plan	A wide range of benefits, including: disability benefits, widow's benefits, life insurance and accidental death and dismemberment benefits, health care, dental and vision benefits.

Collective bargaining agreement expires on December 11, 2011

National Hockey League

Headquarters		Union	
National Hockey League 1251 Avenue of the Americas New York, NY 10020 (212) 789-2000 NHL.com		The National Hockey League Players Assn. 777 Bay Street, Suite 2400 Toronto, Ontario, Canada, M5G 2C8 (416) 408-4040 NHLPA.com	
Leader	**Commissioner** Gary Bettman	No current executive director (since May 2007)	
Roster Spots	23 minimum	**Salaries as % of total revenues**	54% of hockey related income

Minimum Salary
$475,000 in 2007-08 and 2008-09, $500,000 in 2009-10 and 2010-11, $525,000 in 2011-12

Free Agency Eligibility
Unrestricted free agency for players 28 years old with 4 years of service or any player with 7 years of NHL service. Players no longer considered "entry level" players (players between the ages of 18 and 21 are entry level for their first 3 NHL seasons; ages 22 to 23 are entry level for 2 years; age 24 or more for a single year) but who are not eligible for unrestricted free agency are restricted free agents when their contracts expire.

Benefits	
Pension Plan	Players are eligible for pension plan after playing one game in the NHL. Goalies are eligible after one game dressed, but not required to play.
Disabled Players	Players forced to retire because of hockey-related injuries receive benefits of the pension plan in addition to contributions from the NHL Players Emergency Assistance Fund.

Collective bargaining agreement expires on September 15, 2011
The NHLPA has an option to reopen the agreement after 2008-09, or extend it for an extra year after 2010-11.

National Assn. for Stock Car Auto Racing (NASCAR)

Headquarters
National Assn. for Stock Car Auto Racing 1801 W. International Speedway Daytona Beach, FL 32114 (386) 253-0611 NASCAR.com

Leader	CEO Brian France

Major League Soccer (MLS)

Headquarters	Union
Major League Soccer 420 Fifth Avenue, Seventh Floor New York, NY 10018 (212) 450-1200 MLSnet.com	Major League Soccer Players Union 7605 Arlington Road, Suite 250 Bethesda, MD 20814 (301) 718-7273 MLSPlayers.org

Leader	Commissioner Don Garber	MLSPU Executive Director Bob Foose

Collective bargaining agreement expires on January 31, 2010

Arena Football League (AFL)

Headquarters	Union
Arena Football League 105 Madison Avenue, 9th Floor New York, NY 10016 (212) 252-8100 Arenafootball.com	Arena Football League Players Assn. 2021 L Street, NW, Suite 600 Washington, DC 20036 (800) 372-2000, (202) 463-2200 AFLPlayers.org

Leader	Commissioner David Baker	AFLPA Executive Director Gene Upshaw

Collective Bargaining Agreement runs through 2010

Professional Golf Assn. (PGA) Tour

Headquarters
Professional Golf Assn. Tour 100 PGA Tour Boulevard Ponte Vedra Beach, FL 32082 (904) 285-3700 PGATour.com

Leader	Commissioner Tim Finchem

Ladies Professional Golf Assn. (LPGA)

Headquarters	
Ladies Professional Golf Assn. 100 International Golf Drive Daytona Beach, Florida 32124-1092 (386) 274-6200 LPGA.com	
Leader	**Commissioner** Carolyn Bivens

Women's Tennis Assn. (WTA)

Headquarters	
Women's Tennis Assn. One Progress Plaza, Suite 1500 St. Petersburg, FL 33701 (727) 895-5000 SonyEricssonWTATour.com	
Leader	**CEO** Larry Scott

Assn. of Tennis Professionals (ATP)

Headquarters	
Assn. of Tennis Professionals 201 ATP Tour Boulevard Ponte Vedra Beach, FL 32082 (904) 285-8000 ATPTennis.com	
Leader	**Executive Chairman** Etienne de Villiers

Assn. of Volleyball Professionals (AVP)

Headquarters	
AVP Pro Beach Volleyball Tour 6100 Center Drive, 9th Floor Los Angeles, CA 90045 (310) 426-8000 AVP.com	
Leader	**Commissioner** Leonard Armato

Appendix B: Source Notes

Note from author

1   **"You had better learn how to play the game..."**: *North Dallas Forty.*
Written by Peter Gent. Paramount Studios (1979).

Chapter 1

7   **"I am not a businessman..."**: *Diamonds From Sierra Leone.* Song by
Kanye West featuring Jay-Z. Roc-a-Fella Records (2005).

9   **"Steve Young...failed to deposit several paychecks..."**: Steve Young
speech at Roy Firestone Award Dinner honoring Steve Young. Los
Angeles (Nov. 15, 2005).

Chapter 2

15   **"As soon as you give a player money..."**: Craig Neff, "Den of Vipers,"
Sports Illustrated (Oct. 19, 1987).

15   **"There's a 100% chance..."**: Craig Neff, "In Hot and Heavy Pursuit:
Chasing after Clients, Agents Are Able to Use Every Trick in the Book,"
Sports Illustrated (Oct. 19, 1987).

16   **"Getting paid to find gold"**: *The Treasure of the Sierra Madre.* Dir. John
Huston. RCA Pictures (1948).

17   **"The NCAA has strict rules regarding [agent] relationships..."**:
NCAA.org has additional information on NCAA rules governing
agents, listed under "Agents and Amateurism."

18   **"Agents with mob muscle"**: Bruce Selcraig, "The Deal Went Sour," *Sports
Illustrated* (Sept. 15, 1988). See also, Chris Mortensen, *Playing for Keeps:
How One Man Kept the Mob from Sinking Its Hooks into Pro Football.*
Simon & Schuster (1991).

19   **"A Guide to a Career in Professional Athletics"**: National Collegiate
Athletic Assn., 2004-05.
<http://www.ncaa.org/library/general/career_in_pro_athletics/2004-
05/2004-05_career_pro_athletics.pdf>

19   **"Uniform Amateur Agent Act (UAAA)"**: Check NCAA.org for latest
information on UAAA, listed under "Agents and Amateurism."

20   **"The athletes stuck me with the check"**: Mel Levine, *Life in the
Trash Lane: Cash, Cars and Corruption: A Sports Agent's True Story.*
Distinctive Publishing (1993).

21   **"Reason #968 to follow NCAA extra benefits rules"**: Charles Robinson,
"Attorney's Letter Says Bush Family Got $100,000." *Yahoo! Sports*
(April 29, 2006).

Chapter 3

24   **"According to a 2004 study by the American Council on Education…"**: American Council on Education (ACE). "Credit card ownership and behavior among traditional-age undergraduates (2003-04)."

25   **"Your eligibility is your most valuable asset"**: Ryan Nece. Personal interview (June 13, 2006).

26   **"The NCAA declined to tell me how many claims have been paid out…"**: E-mail: from NCAA spokesman Erik Christianson: "QUESTION: How many policies have paid out? ANSWER: We are not allowed to disclose this information" (Feb. 20, 2007). In subsequent emails, Christianson cited confidentiality concerns and agreements with its insurance providers. In *Freakonomics*, authors Steven Levitt and Stephen Dubner observe the following: "In the late 1990s, price of term insurance fell dramatically. This passed as something of a mystery, for the decline had no obvious cause…So what happened? The Internet happened…Suddenly customers were paying $1 billion less a year for term life insurance. Insurance prices [are] less a secret than a set of facts dispensed in a way that made comparisons difficult. Information is a beacon, a cudgel, an olive branch—all depending on who wields it and how."

26   **"Ed Chester…collected $1 million on a policy"**: Gary Klein, "Premium Players: Insurance Policies Are Becoming Standard for Elite College Athletes." *Los Angeles Times* (Feb. 20, 2005).

26   **"An athlete's disability policy from Lloyd's of London states…"**: Jeff Rabjohns, "Playing It Safe—at a Price." *Indianapolis Star* (Feb. 1, 2005).

Chapter 4

29   **"The goal should not be to get to the NBA…"**: Jerry West on a Los Angeles sports talk radio show. Confirmed quote with Mr. West at Pauley Pavilion on Jan. 21, 2006.

29   **"Why is it nobody asks…"**: Pete Williams, *The Draft: A Year Inside the NFL's Search for Talent*. St. Martin's Griffin (2006).

31   **"I am not saying I'm ready…"**: Ndudi Ebi quoted. Lute Olson, *Lute!: The Seasons of My Life*. Thomas Dunne Books (2006).

32   **"Former UNC coach Dean Smith…"**: Filip Bondy, *Tip-Off: How the 1984 NBA Draft Changed Basketball Forever*. Da Capo Press (2007).

32   **"Memphis basketball coach John Calipari famously tore up…"**: Alex French, "Is This the Most Powerful Man in Sports?" *Gentleman's Quarterly* (July 2007). Also, Jason Lloyd, "Matta Free to Talk with Wildcats." *The Morning Journal* (March 24, 2007).

33   **"Declaring for the NFL Draft"**: Jack Mills via e-mail (July 2, 2007).

Chapter 5

35 **"A lot of players didn't have agents..."**: Terry Bradshaw, *It's Only a Game*. Pocket Books (2002).

36 **"Self-serving...incompetent...criminal"**: Craig Neff, "Den of Vipers." *Sports Illustrated* (Oct. 19, 1987).

36 **"...all agents are sleazebags..."**: Michael Wright, "Sleazy Agents? Most Are Honorable, Ethical." *Sports Business Journal* (Oct. 14, 2002).

29 **"Agent as NBA draft guide"**: Jonathan Givony, "Navigating through the NBA Agent Selection Process." *DraftExpress.com* (April 13, 2007). <http://www.draftexpress.com/viewarticle.php?a=1997>

38 **"More NBPA certified player agents."** Number of certified player agents confirmed by NBPA via e-mail (July 31, 2007).

38 **"In 1963, Green Bay Packer Jim Ringo brought a lawyer..."**: Ken Shropshire and Timothy Davis, *The Business of Sports Agents*. University of Pennsylvania Press (2003). Story has been widely reported.

38 **"The top 16 agents represent 252 players."**: Calculated on *Hoopshype.com*, <http://www.hoopshype.com/agents.htm>

39 **"[Grant Hill] reportedly paid lawyer Lon Babby $350,000."**: Liz Mullen, "Babby Signs Battier." *Sports Business Journal* (May 14–20, 2001).

39 **"The MLBPA is nothing if not consistent..."**: MLBPA.com, visited August 25, 2007, <http://mlbplayers.mlb.com/pa/info/faq.jsp>

43 **"Increase the chance you will get qualified representation"**: Adonal Foyle, NBA player. Personal interview (Aug. 8, 2006).

Chapter 6

General notes: Information about amateur drafts obtained from league and players association Web sites. If you are a college athlete or parent, visit NCAA.org and also your athletic department's Web site for rules, policies and state laws regarding eligibility and sports agents.

45 **"Draft day is not important..."**: Peter King, "Old School." *Sports Illustrated* (April 23, 2007).

50 **"I'm back..."**: Read more on Randolph Morris' unusual path to the NBA on author's blog, <http://moneyplayers.typepad.com/blog/2006/12/still_morris_th.html>

Chapter 7

52   **"book on mastering the 40-yard dash..."** Mark Gough, *Mastering the 40 Yard Dash*. Athletic Edge Sports

54   **"Big Brother is watching"**: Michael Bamberger and Don Yaeger, "NFL Security: Big Brother is Watching." *Sports Illustrated* (April 15, 1996).

55   **From the NBA to Europe...**: Tyus Edney. Personal interview (Aug. 10, 2007).

Chapter 8

Business talk: Wikipedia.com is an excellent starting point to learn more about business terms. I also recommend: Jack Friedman, Dictionary of Business Terms, Barron's Educational Series (fourth edition, 2007).

Chapter 9

67   **"Show me the money"**: *Jerry Maguire*. Dir. Cameron Crowe. Sony Pictures (1996).

68   **"Business managers operate outside the legal jurisdiction of players associations."**: James Paton, "Suit by Nene Claims Ex-Manager Was Flop." *Rocky Mountain News* (Aug. 1, 2007).

Chapter 10

71   **"Believe nothing..."**: Gautama Siddharta, founder of Buddhism (563–483 BC).

72   **"We are artful liars"**: Sam Antar. Personal interview (March 8, 2007). Also, Herb Greenberg, "My Lunch With 2 Fraudsters: Food for Thought for Investors." *The Wall Street Journal* (March 3, 2007).

73   **"Where the money is"**: Marc Isenberg, "Pro Athletes Must Use Caution to Avoid Financial Runaround." *Sports Business Journal* (Aug. 28, 2006). Material in this section borrows liberally from my *Sports Business Journal* article about financial fraudster Kirk Wright and the lessons learned.

73   **"Where the money is"**: The famous response given by notorious bank robber Willie Sutton, when asked why he robs banks. In Sutton's autobiography, *Where the Money Was: The Memoirs of a Bank Robber*. Viking Press (1976). Sutton denies he ever said this, saying it belongs to a writer named Mitch Ohnstad.

73   **"According to NFL Players Association...players lost...$42 million"**: Edward Pound and Douglas Pasternak, "Money Players: How some of the NFL's biggest stars got taken for millions." *US News & World Report* (Feb. 3, 2002).

74 **"Don't jump into hedge funds"**: The current SEC requirements for accredited investors have been in place since 1982. In December 2006 the SEC proposed increasing minimum required to invest in hedge funds to "at least $2.5 million in assets, excluding the value of their primary residence," rather than $1 million in assets (including value of their home) currently required. The new investment minimum would be adjusted for inflation every five years. As I suggested, whatever the threshold, investors can self-impose their own minimum.

76 **"The following questions and comments are based..."**: National Futures Assn. "Investment Swindles: How They Work and How to Avoid Them." (1998). <www.nfa.futures.org/investor/inv_swindles/ InvestmentSwindles1998.pdf>

Chapter 11

79 **"It's the greed of the sucker..."**: David Spanier, *Total Poker*. Fireside (1977)

80 **"Benjamin Graham wrote..."**: Benjamin Graham, *The Intelligent Investor: The Definitive Book on Value Investing*. HarperBusiness (revised edition 2003).

80 **"The Original Ponzi Scheme"**: Mitchell Zuckoff, *Ponzi's Scheme: The True Story of a Financial Legend*. (Random House, 2006). Also, search "Charles Ponzi" and "Ponzi schemes" on wikipedia.com.

81 **"Steep tuition for crash course..."**: John Papanek, "A Lot of Hurt." *Sports Illustrated* (Oct. 19, 1987).

81 **"He was a good guy."**: Charles Barkley with Roy Johnson. *Outrageous!: The Fine Life and Flagrant Good Times of Basketball's Irresistible Force*. Simon & Schuster (1992). Interestingly, Barkley claimed he was misquoted in this book, Barkley's autobiography, but it is still good advice.

82 **"Agent churns former teammate"**: Edward Pound and Douglas Pasternak, "Money Players: How Some of the NFL's Biggest Stars Got Taken for Millions." *US News & World Report* (Feb. 3, 2002).

82 **"Friends don't let friends rip them off"**: ibid

83 **"Financial adviser gambling heavily?"**: ibid.

83 **"Let's hope "U can't touch this"**: wikipedia.com: <http://en.wikipedia. org/wiki/MC_Hammer>

Chapter 12

87 **"Neither a borrower nor a lender be..."**: William Shakespeare, *Hamlet*. Stationers Company (1623). The line was spoken by Polonius, who was the adviser to Claudius (King of Denmark).

87 **"Burton Malkiel gives an example of twin brothers who invest…"**
Burton Malkiel, *The Random Walk Guide to Investing.* W. W. Norton
(1973, ninth edition)

88 **"You knew how to get by in college"**: Tyus Edney. Personal interview
(Aug. 10, 2007).

89 **"Be able to do what you want"**: Jack Mills. Via e-mail (July 12, 2007).

93 **"Neither a borrower nor a lender be"**: Anonymous NBA player.
Personal interview (August 12, 2007). In order to keep peace in his
family, he requested that I not use his name.

94 **"The greatest of all time"**: Thomas Hauser, *Muhammad Ali: His Life and
Times.* Simon & Schuster (1991).

Chapter 15

Note: Richard Greene, a tax and estate attorney, assisted greatly with
this chapter.

113 **"Pete Rose was hit with a $154,000 tax bill…"**: Robert Anglen, "Further
Tax Woes for Pete Rose." *The Cincinnati Enquirer* (Jan. 24, 2003).

114 **Residency and state taxes**: For state income taxes in each state, check:
<http://www.taxadmin.org/fta/rate/ind_inc.html>

114 **"according to a Tax Foundation report…"**: Rick Vander Knyff, "Could
You Be Hit By the 'Jock Tax'?" *MSN Money* (undated).

116 **"Road to nowhere."**: Rick Telander, "A Troubling Tale: 7 kids, 5 Moms
and 1 Absent Dad," *Chicago Sun-Times* (Feb 25, 2000).

Chapter 17

129 **"Cure the common cold, get banned"**: Chris Colston, "Hassles,
Indignities Come with NFL Drug Testing." *USA Today* (June 28, 2006).

Chapter 18

133 **"If there is no struggle there is no progress…"**: "What, to the Slave, is
the Fourth of July?" Frederick Douglas speech (1852).

133 **"Quoted by Curt Flood…"**: Curt Flood, *The Way It Is.* Trident
Press (1971).

134 **"Professional athletes as property…"**: Brad Snyder. *A Well-Paid Slave:
Curt Flood's Fight for Free Agency in Professional Sports.* Viking
Adult (2006).

135 **"MLB Commissioner Bud Selig apologized for the reserve clause…"**
Selig quoted at Sports Lawyers Conference annual conference
(May 17, 2007).

135 **"If there were a pro athletes hall of fame…"**: Marc Isenberg, "Book
Brings Flood's Contribution to Game Out of the Shadows." *Sports
Business Journal* (May 14, 2007).

138 **"I want to thank Spencer Haywood…"**: Jayda Evans, "A Long Rise Back for Spencer Haywood." *Seattle Times* (Feb. 25, 2007).

Chapter 19

144 **"$50,000 backups and $40,000 starters."**: Gordon Forbes, "1982 Strike Changed Salaries Forever." *USA Today* (June 8, 2001).

146 **"Miller 'as important to the history of baseball as Jackie Robinson.'"**: Marvin Miller, *A Whole Different Ball Game: The Inside Story of the Baseball Revolution*. Ivan R. Dee (1991).

Chapter 20

154 **"In 2006, the New York Yankees generated revenue of $302 million…"** *Forbes* (April 19, 2007). Available at: <http://www.forbes.com/lists/2007/33/07mlb_The-Business-Of-Baseball_Rank.html>

154 **"Bill Walton, who was broadcasting the game for ESPN, said…"**: Chris McCosky, "Pistons-Pacers Brawl Spills into the Stands." *The Detroit News* (Nov. 20, 2004).

155 **"In April 2007, the NFL inaugurated sanctions for conduct…"**: "Highlights of NFL's Revised Conduct Policy." *USA Today* (April 10, 2007).

Chapter 21

159 **"Kaiser Family Foundation survey…"**: Kaiser Family Foundation National Survey of Kids (and Their Parents) About Famous Athletes as Role Models" (Oct. 12, 2000). <http://www.kff.org/kaiserpolls/3070-index.cfm>

160 Note: Advice from T.J. Simers, Robert Lipsyte, Art Spander, Fred Claire, Alexander Wolff, Len Elmore and Shelley Smith all sent to author via e-mail.

Chapter 22

168 **"Teams see player philanthropy as critical…"**: Bruce Knecht, "Big Players in Charity." *The Wall Steet Journal* (April 28, 2007).

Chapter 23

174 **"More than Magic"**: Earvin Johnson speech. Collegiate Business Conference (Aug. 3, 2007).

174 **"A Forbes article…"** Robert La Franco, "The Magic and the money." *Forbes* (Dec, 16, 1996).

175 **"Ralph Cindrich, sports agent, former NFL player"**: E-mail from Ralph Cindrich (March 13, 2007).

175 **"Steve Kerr, general manager, Phoenix Suns, five-time NBA champion"**: E-mail from Steve Kerr, general manager, Phoenix Suns, five-time NBA (March 2, 2007).

176 **"Charles Barkley, TNT analyst, NBA Hall of Famer"**: Charles Barkley with Roy Johnson. *Outrageous!: The Fine Life and Flagrant Good Times of Basketball's Irresistible Force.* Simon & Schuster (1992).

177 **"Curtis Martin, former NFL star running back"**: Interview by Bill King, "Former NFLer Curtis Martin Discusses Character Issues In Sports." *Sports Business Journal* (Sept. 19, 2007).

177 **"Danny Ainge, general manager, Boston Celtics, former NBA player"**: Interview. Danny Ainge (July 22, 2002).

178 **"10 Challenges of Retirement"**: Written by Ken Ruettgers. Used with his permission.

About the Author

Marc Isenberg is a nationally known writer and author on the business of sports. He founded A-Game, LLC, a company that provides educational materials and programs for the sports community. Marc passionately studied Bull and Bear markets while growing up in a Chicago suburb. He earned his undergraduate degree from Emory University in Atlanta, where he played on the men's basketball team, and his MBA from The Paul Merage School of Business at UC Irvine. Marc is the co-author of *The Student-Athlete Survival Guide* (McGraw Hill 2001) and *The Truth about Gambling* (A-Game 2003). He has been a guest on ESPN's *Outside the Lines*, and his articles have appeared in *The New York Times, Street & Smith's Sports Business Journal, The NCAA News* and *Chicago Sun-Times*. Marc is on the NCAA-approved-speakers list and has been a frequent guest lecturer on sports and business issues at universities, including UCLA and USC. He works as a business and financial consultant in Santa Monica, Calif., where he lives with his wife, Debbie Spander. He can be reached at marc.isenberg@gmail.com.

Visit the author's blog at **moneyplayers.typepad.com**.